The
Wives
of the
Berkeleys

The Wives of the Berkeleys

*Families and Marriage
in Tudor and Stuart England*

XMERA LTD

First published in the United Kingdom
by Xmera Ltd in 2021

Copyright © Jan Broadway

All rights reserved. No part of this publication may be reproduced or transmitted in any form or by an means, electronic or mechanical including photocopying, recording or any information storage or retrieval system, without prior permission in writing from the publishers.

ISBN 978-0-9567428-1-0

Contents

	Preface	vii
	Note to the Reader	ix
	Family Trees	x
1	The Savage Marriage	1
2	A Widow and her Children	23
3	Mary Queen of Scots and the Howards	42
4	Careys and Townshends	60
5	Cokes and Stanhopes	76
6	End of an Era	87
	Notes	92
	Index	96

Preface

It is now more than a quarter of a century since I first read the history of the Berkeleys written by John Smyth of Nibley in the early seventeenth century. Thanks to his work we know more about this comparatively obscure baronial family across over four centuries than perhaps any other non-royal dynasty. The *Lives of the Berkeleys* (edited by Sir John Maclean in the late nineteenth century) was a detailed, thorough account that drew on Smyth's decades of working with the relevant archives as the family's man-of-business. It is an account that takes a determinedly patrilineal approach to his subject, structuring it around the life of the successive lords and describing the lives of their wives and children only within the context of the family. This patrilineal approach to family history remains dominant, even in the twenty-first century. Katharine Howard, wife of Henry, lord Berkeley, has only one entry in the index of a modern account of her birth family.

Increasingly scholars are recognising the importance of the role of women in dynastic history. As the bringers of wealth at marriage, bearers of children and managers of estates in the absence of their husbands, women played an important part in the fortunes of aristocratic families and a patrilineal approach obscures the multi-dimensional relationships that existed within the English aristocracy. A recent study of the Tudor Howards by Nicola Clark explores the role of the women who were either born into or through marriage joined the dynasty. Such a wider perspective is particularly relevant for looking at the last century of Smyth's account of the Berkeley lords, for during this period the nominal head of the family was mostly either a minor, absent or willing to concede authority to his wife or mother. It was also largely due to their wives that from early in Elizabeth I's reign the Berkeleys ceased to maintain their principal residence in Gloucestershire, moving initially to Warwickshire and later to Surrey. Berkeley castle remained an important symbol of their lineage, but it was a place for occasional visits not to live in.

The aristocracy and leading gentry of Tudor and Stuart England were a small, socially cohesive, heavily inter-related group. Any two individuals within it can almost invariably be shown to be linked with far fewer than six degrees of separation. Marital ties were visually recorded in coats of arms, which when engraved in silver, wood and stone reminded generations of distant cousins of their kinship. Ceremonial events such as coronations, the opening of parliament and funerals provided regular opportunities for the community to present itself in public. This was a community where individuals knew where they stood and who their relations were, although the exact degree of their kinship might have been forgotten. Tracing kinship circles presents the historian with a number of challenges. Apart from the patchy survival of archival evidence, the most significant hurdle is the frequency with which the same name occurs within a family. I apologise in advance to readers for the confusion that arises when, for example, between 1614 and 1635 both George, lord Berkeley's mother and his wife were called Lady Elizabeth Berkeley.

In his account of the Berkeley lords John Smyth criticised the wives of the last four generations of having 'had private ends for their own advantages upon their husbands affaires' and for having 'too often prevailed over them'. In what follows, I have tried to tell the story of the Tudor and Stuart Berkeleys from a perspective, that takes into account the wider concerns of those maligned wives. Those concerns expanded beyond the immediate succession of the Berkeley barony to encompass younger sons and daughters, children from previous marriages, siblings, nieces and nephews, cousins – the entire multi-dimensional network of kinship ties within which they lived their lives. By this collective biography I hope to convince the reader that Smyth's judgement was unfair and that the problems of the Berkeley family were not all the fault of their wives.

~~~

I have been researching and writing this book intermittently over a long period and have received assistance and encouragement from many people, for which I am very grateful. I should particularly mention Richard Cust, who first suggested that I should look at the volumes of John Smyth's papers more than a quarter of a century ago. The volumes were then in Gloucester Library, but have since moved to Gloucestershire Archives. The staff of both institutions have been extremely helpful over the years. The former Gloucestershire county archivist Mr John Smith arranged for me to visit the Berkeley Castle archive, where I was able to examine Smyth's original manuscript. Working with the much missed Lisa Jardine and all those associated with the Centre for Editing Lives and Letters, then at Queen Mary, encouraged my engagement with biographical history. Diarmuid MacCulloch was kind enough to send me research notes on Lady Anne Berkeley. I gave a preliminary presentation of my research on Lady Anne at the Gloucester History Festival under the auspices of an event organized by John Chandler for the Gloucestershire County History Trust. My fellow trustees and the editors and volunteers working on producing further volumes for *VCH Gloucestershire* and various members of the Bristol and Gloucestershire Archaeological Society have provided the research support network I needed, having abandoned full-time academic life. My greatest debt is as ever to Alan Cursue, to whom I can only apologise for once again not having written about pirates.

Note to the Reader

All dates are in the Old Style (Julian) calendar, but I have adhered to the modern practice of dating years from 1 January. I have made no attempt to give modern equivalents for sums of money.

A number of family trees are included, in an effort to assist the reader in keeping track of the various Elizabeths, Katherines, Williams, Georges etc. mentioned in the text. These are greatly simplified, omitting some spouses and numerous siblings, in the hope of increasing clarity.

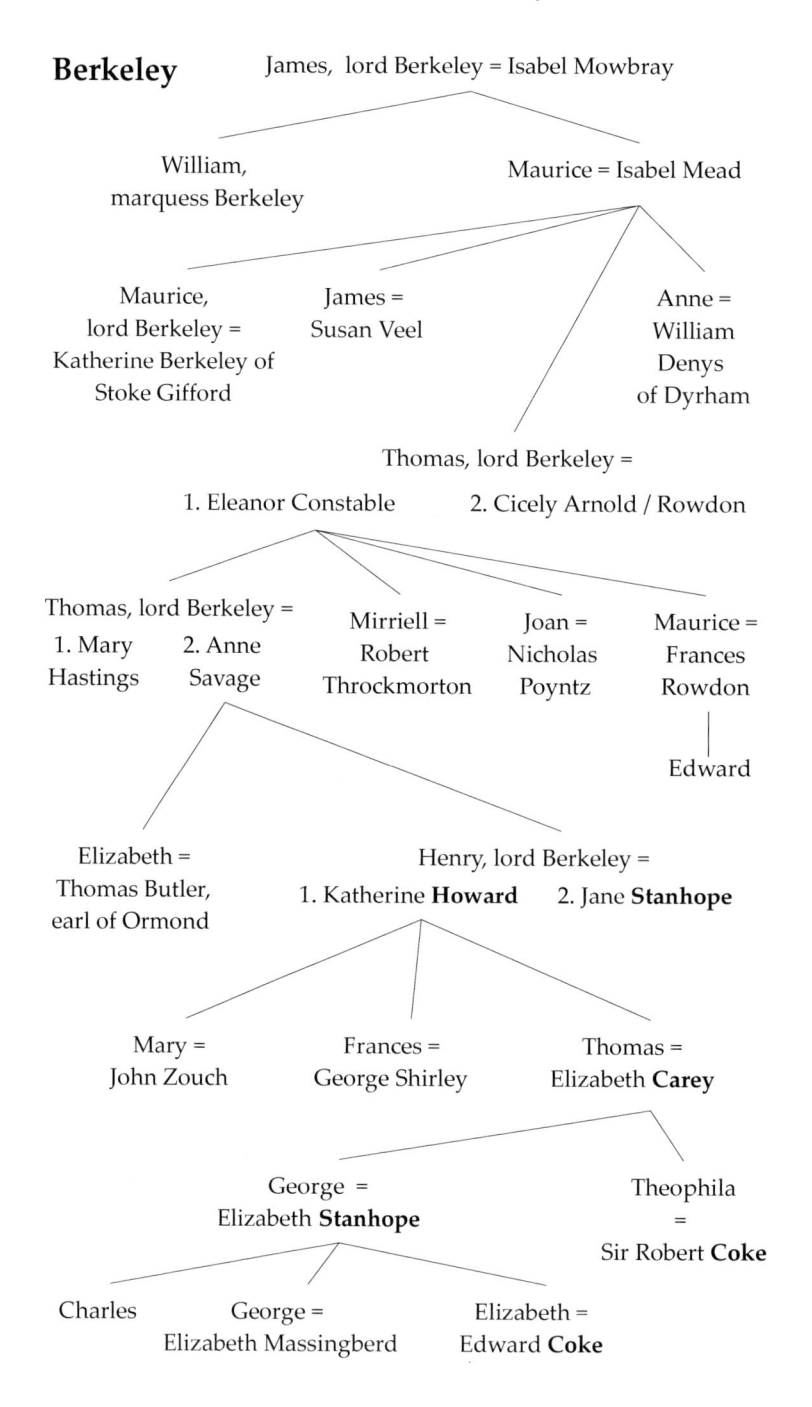

Wives of the Berkeleys

Berkeley

James, lord Berkeley = Isabel Mowbray

- William, marquess Berkeley
- Maurice = Isabel Mead
  - Maurice, lord Berkeley = Katherine Berkeley of Stoke Gifford
  - James = Susan Veel
  - Anne = William Denys of Dyrham

Thomas, lord Berkeley =
1. Eleanor Constable   2. Cicely Arnold / Rowdon

- Thomas, lord Berkeley = 1. Mary Hastings 2. Anne Savage
- Mirriell = Robert Throckmorton
- Joan = Nicholas Poyntz
- Maurice = Frances Rowdon
  - Edward

- Elizabeth = Thomas Butler, earl of Ormond
- Henry, lord Berkeley = 1. Katherine **Howard**   2. Jane **Stanhope**
  - Mary = John Zouch
  - Frances = George Shirley
  - Thomas = Elizabeth **Carey**
    - George = Elizabeth **Stanhope**
      - Charles
      - George = Elizabeth Massingberd
      - Elizabeth = Edward **Coke**
    - Theophila = Sir Robert **Coke**

Howard (1)

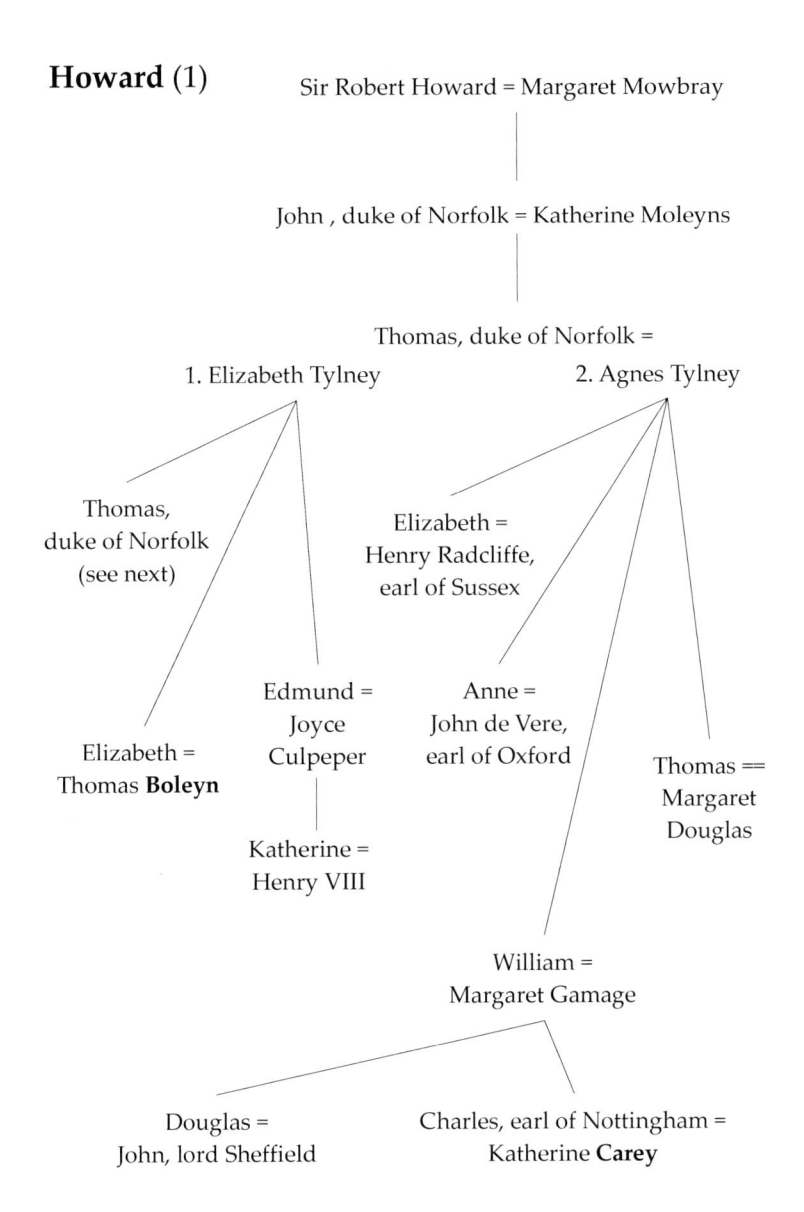

Sir Robert Howard = Margaret Mowbray

John, duke of Norfolk = Katherine Moleyns

Thomas, duke of Norfolk =
1. Elizabeth Tylney   2. Agnes Tylney

Thomas, duke of Norfolk (see next)

Elizabeth = Thomas **Boleyn**

Edmund = Joyce Culpeper

Katherine = Henry VIII

Elizabeth = Henry Radcliffe, earl of Sussex

Anne = John de Vere, earl of Oxford

Thomas == Margaret Douglas

William = Margaret Gamage

Douglas = John, lord Sheffield

Charles, earl of Nottingham = Katherine **Carey**

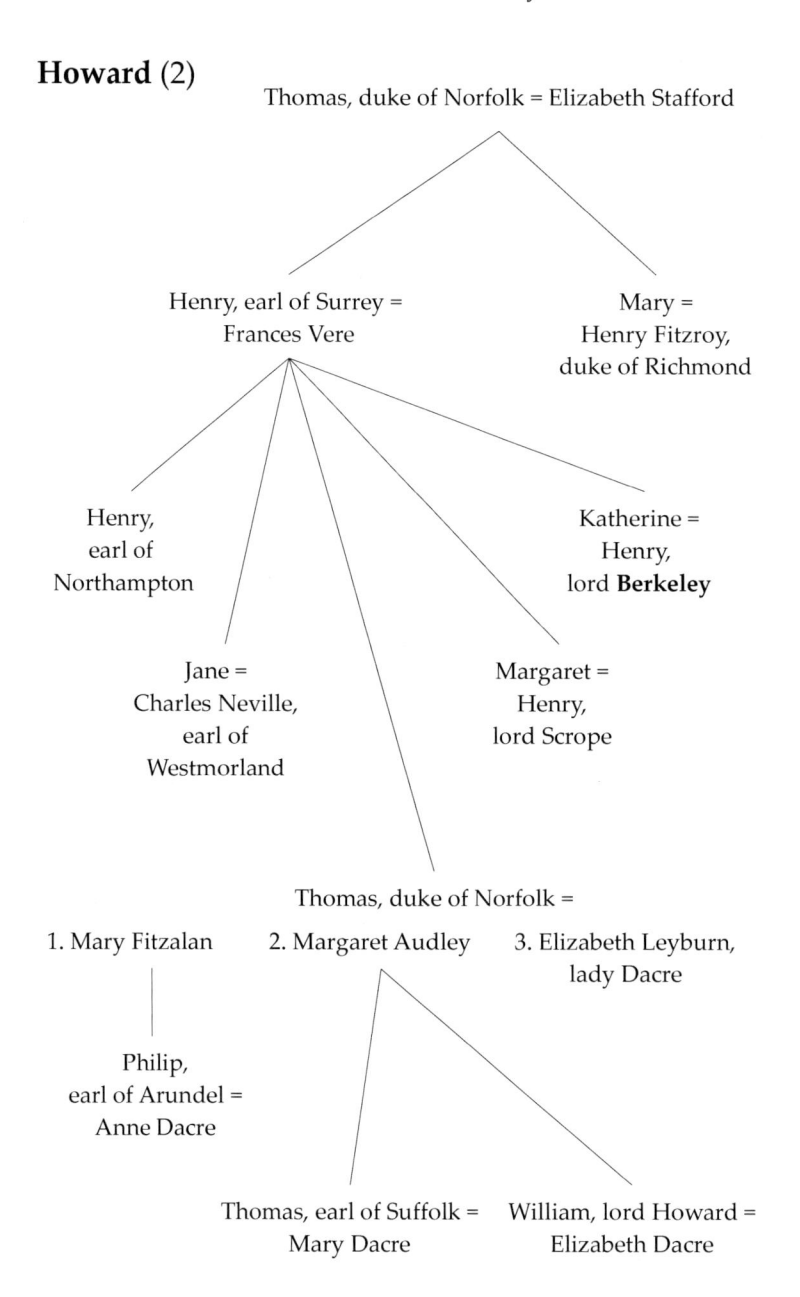

Wives of the Berkeleys

Howard (2)

Thomas, duke of Norfolk = Elizabeth Stafford

- Henry, earl of Surrey = Frances Vere
- Mary = Henry Fitzroy, duke of Richmond

Children of Henry, earl of Surrey and Frances Vere:
- Henry, earl of Northampton
- Jane = Charles Neville, earl of Westmorland
- Katherine = Henry, lord **Berkeley**
- Margaret = Henry, lord Scrope
- Thomas, duke of Norfolk

Thomas, duke of Norfolk =
1. Mary Fitzalan
2. Margaret Audley
3. Elizabeth Leyburn, lady Dacre

- Philip, earl of Arundel = Anne Dacre (son of Mary Fitzalan)
- Thomas, earl of Suffolk = Mary Dacre (son of Margaret Audley)
- William, lord Howard = Elizabeth Dacre (son of Margaret Audley)

Boleyn/Carey

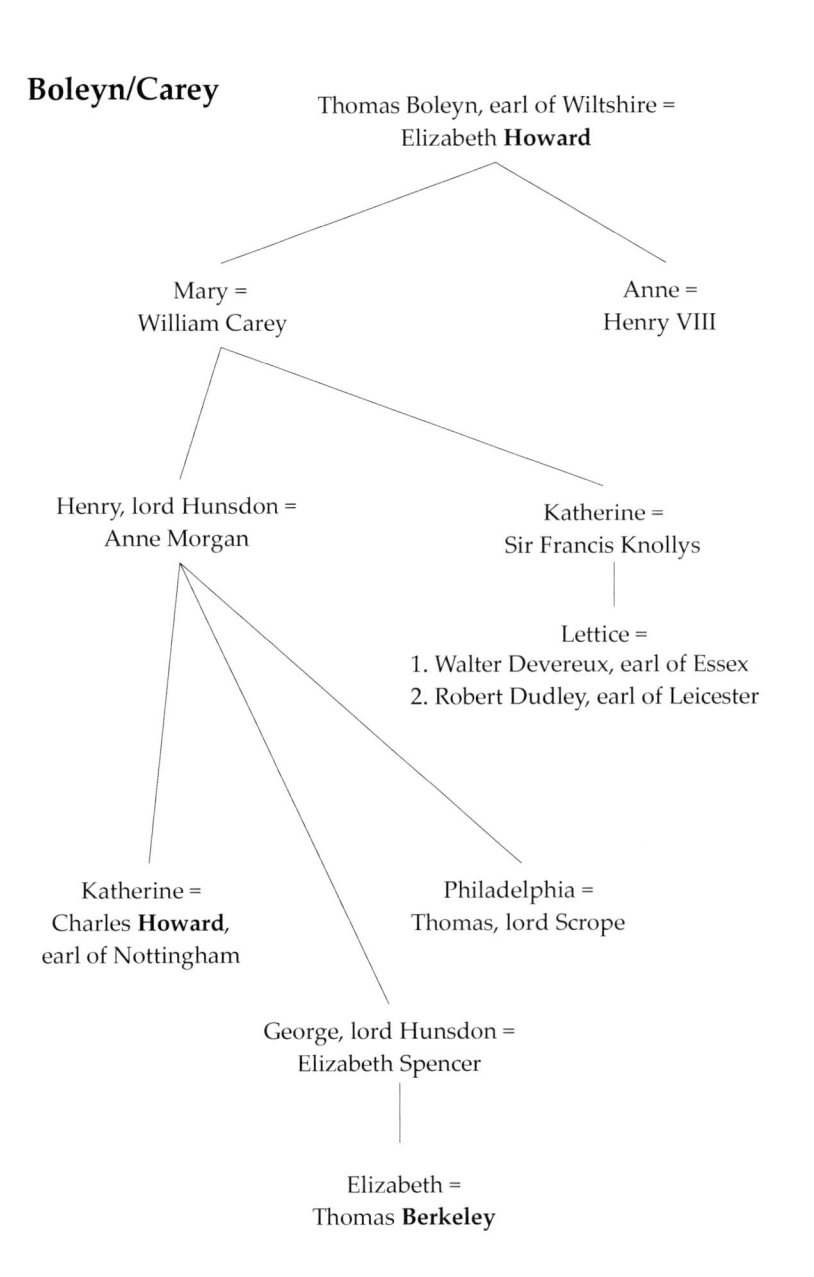

Thomas Boleyn, earl of Wiltshire = Elizabeth **Howard**

- Mary = William Carey
- Anne = Henry VIII

Children of Mary and William Carey:

- Henry, lord Hunsdon = Anne Morgan
- Katherine = Sir Francis Knollys
  - Lettice =
    1. Walter Devereux, earl of Essex
    2. Robert Dudley, earl of Leicester

Children of Henry, lord Hunsdon and Anne Morgan:

- Katherine = Charles **Howard**, earl of Nottingham
- Philadelphia = Thomas, lord Scrope
- George, lord Hunsdon = Elizabeth Spencer
  - Elizabeth = Thomas **Berkeley**

Wives of the Berkeleys

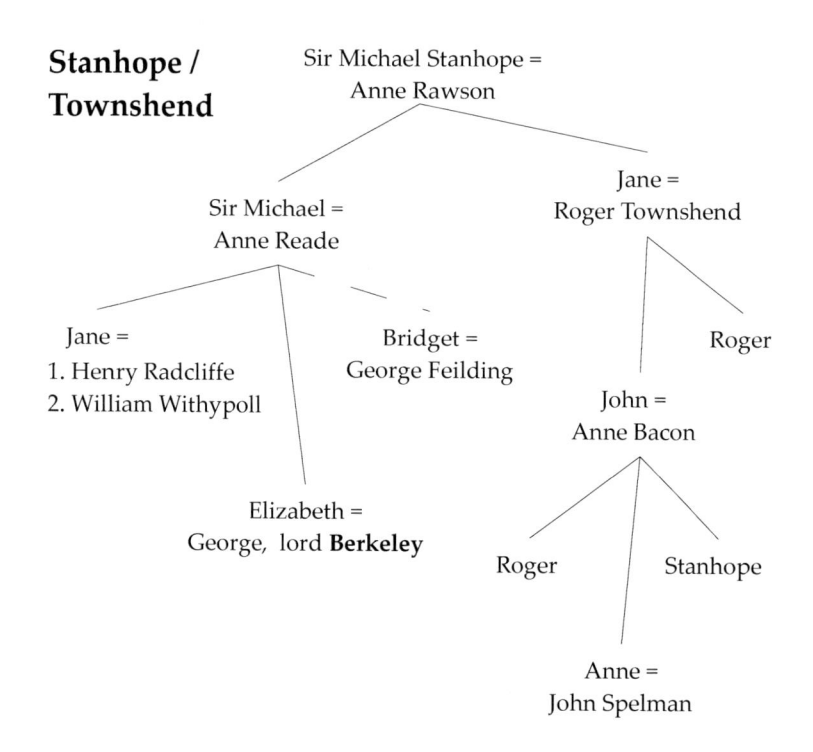

Stanhope / Townshend

Sir Michael Stanhope = Anne Rawson

- Sir Michael = Anne Reade
- Jane = Roger Townshend

Children of Sir Michael and Anne Reade:
- Jane = 1. Henry Radcliffe, 2. William Withypoll
- Bridget = George Feilding
- Elizabeth = George, lord **Berkeley**

Children of Jane and Roger Townshend:
- Roger
- John = Anne Bacon

Children of John and Anne Bacon:
- Roger
- Stanhope
- Anne = John Spelman

Coke

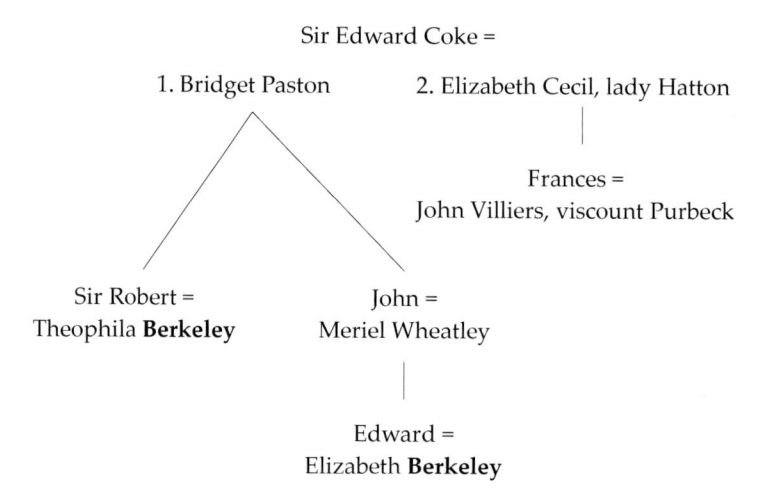

Sir Edward Coke =
1. Bridget Paston
2. Elizabeth Cecil, lady Hatton

Children of Bridget Paston:
- Sir Robert = Theophila **Berkeley**
- John = Meriel Wheatley

Child of Elizabeth Cecil:
- Frances = John Villiers, viscount Purbeck

Child of John and Meriel Wheatley:
- Edward = Elizabeth **Berkeley**

1 The Savage Marriage

Early one morning in late January 1533 Henry VIII and Anne Boleyn slipped away from the court at Greenwich. They were rowed up-river by barge to Westminster, where the old palace stood beside the abbey founded by Edward the Confessor. Just downstream the king's grand new palace of Whitehall was being built along the Thames. There, in a small room above the great gatehouse before a few trusted witnesses, Anne and Henry were married. After years of delay the king and his mistress had been forced into a hurried wedding, when Anne realized she was pregnant. The couple assumed that the child would be a healthy boy, since this would be God's will. When born, the child needed to be legitimate. Henry already had one bastard son in the adolescent Henry, duke of Richmond. Another would be of little use, and embarrassing for a king whose attempts to divorce his wife had been public knowledge for over five years. Yet the marriage had to remain a secret for as long as possible. The king still hoped to persuade the pope to declare his earlier marriage to Catherine of Aragon invalid. This was unlikely to happen, if the pope knew his decision had been pre-empted. Hence the need for a secret ceremony before only a few, discreet and reliable witnesses.

Later that spring a second marriage took place at Henry's court. Anne Savage, one of the gentlewomen in attendance on Anne Boleyn, married an extremely eligible and very recent widower. Of medium build and dark-haired, Anne Savage was not one of the acknowledged court beauties. How, the gossips wondered, had Anne Savage bagged Thomas, lord Berkeley? As news of the king's secret wedding seeped out, the gossips had their answer. It seemed clear to them, that Anne had attended the new queen to her wedding and marriage to Lord Berkeley was her reward. The new Lady Berkeley was certainly a determined and forthright woman, possessing what contemporaries described as a 'masculine spirit'.[1] Clearly, she was not someone who would have baulked at the idea of being witness to a clandestine wedding. Discretion, however, was not one of her abiding characteristics, which made her a less obvious choice. While she may have attended the king's wedding, as we shall see, royal gratitude towards a discreet witness is not the only possible or even most likely explanation for her subsequent marriage.

Wives of the Berkeleys

Anne came from a leading family of Cheshire gentry. The Savages had risen to prominence through their service to successive English kings during the Hundred Years War against France and fought on the Yorkist side in the Wars of the Roses. However, as kinsmen of Lord Stanley, who married the Lancastrian heiress Lady Margaret Beaufort, they were regarded with suspicion by Richard III after he took the throne. In 1485 Anne's grandfather Sir John Savage supported Lady Margaret's son Henry Tudor, when he claimed the throne. Having commanded the left-wing of the Tudor army at Bosworth, Sir John received lands and offices as a reward from the new king. He died in Henry VII's service at the siege of Boulogne in 1492. Sir John's brother Thomas, a cleric and diplomat, was part of the embassy that negotiated the marriage of Catherine of Aragon to Prince Arthur. Rising through the ranks of the church, he became archbishop of York in 1501.

When Anne was growing up, her father Sir John Savage was sheriff, constable of Hanley Castle and steward of Elmley Castle in Worcestershire and steward of Tewkesbury in Gloucestershire. Anne was born around 1506, when her father's career was at its height and she was raised predominantly at Hanley Castle and Tewkesbury. She grew up as part of a large family with seven brothers. There may have been sisters as well, although none are recorded in the family pedigree. (It was only Anne's marriage to a peer, that ensured she was remembered by later generations of her family.) An obvious sign of her father's success in the service of the Tudors was that his eldest son, another John, married Elizabeth, the daughter of Charles Somerset, lord Herbert. Lord Herbert was the illegitimate son of Henry Beaufort, duke of Somerset and first cousin of Lady Margaret Beaufort. Lord Herbert was a prominent member of Henry VII's court and one of the king's councillors. Under Henry VIII he became chamberlain, the nominal head of the king's household, and in 1514 was created Earl of Worcester. Marriage to the daughter of a peer linked to the royal family was a prestigious match for Anne's brother and a mark of her father's status at the time.

In 1516 Anne's world fell apart. Her father had already clashed with Cardinal Wolsey, the king's leading minister, over Sir John's lack of regard for the law in exercising his authority as sheriff. Sir John had grown up in an environment, where might was right and power was exercised by local magnates through the sword not the courts. He carried this militaristic ethos on into the reign of Henry VIII. Wolsey meanwhile was determined to establish the authority of the central bureaucracy and law courts throughout the country. In 1516 the cardinal got his chance to act against Sir John, when Anne's brother John and the Savage henchmen went too far. They set upon and killed John Pauncefote, a local magistrate, when he was waiting to cross the Severn by ferry to attend the quarter sessions at Cirencester. The exact nature of the dispute between Pauncefote and the Savages is unclear, but the murder of a justice of the peace on his way to the sessions was the sort of flagrant breach of the king's peace that Wolsey was determined to prosecute. Sir John was stripped of his offices and sent with his son to the Tower. Once her father and brother were no longer around to intimidate people, further complainants came forward. By the time they came to trial the following year at least sixty-seven indictments had been amassed against them. The Savages were used as an example, to dissuade other local officials from exercising power and using intimidation in their own rather than the king's interest.

It is not certain where Anne was living at the time of her father's arrest. At ten years of age and with her mother having apparently died before Sir John's downfall, she may already have been sent to join a higher status household as part of her education. If not, then a new home would have been found for her, following the arrests. It seems most likely that she joined the household of her sister-in-law's father, the earl of Worcester. John Savage and Elizabeth Somerset had been contracted to marry as young children, with the actual wedding taking place once Elizabeth was twelve, the age of legal maturity for girls. They would not have co-habited for several years after that and, as by 1516 the couple had no children, Elizabeth was probably still living in her father's household.

After a long series of hearings Sir John and his son were convicted. The Earl of Worcester then worked tirelessly to secure them pardons from the king. In this the earl was helped by the king's sister Mary, duchess of Suffolk. In 1514 Worcester had accompanied Mary to Paris and remained in France throughout her brief marriage to Louis XII. Following the king's death, Mary married Charles Brandon, duke of Suffolk, who had been sent to accompany her back to England. The king's anger over this precipitate, though not unexpected, marriage, was directed at Worcester as well as the duke and duchess. The bond created by this shared experience inclined the duchess to help Worcester obtain a pardon for his son-in-law. Negotiating a pardon took time, as the king and Wolsey were determined to exact as much money from the transaction as they could. This was both to ensure that the fate of the Savages acted as a deterrent to others and to help replenish the coffers after their recent military campaigns in France. Once agreed, there was a tortuous bureaucratic process for the pardon to go through before it was fully ratified. This meant paying fees and gratuities to various officials in addition to the actual fines. Finally in 1520 Sir John and his son had their sealed pardons and were able to resume their lives. The cost however was enormous. Anne was now of marriageable age, but there was little money left to provide her with a dowry.

With the prospect of only a meagre dowry Anne's options were limited. She might have returned to her father's household, hoping to attract a proposal from a local gentleman or merchant more interested in her pedigree than her wealth. In 1521 her father sought to restore his own fortunes by marrying again. His new wife, Alice, was the widow and executrix of Sir William Gresley, with whom she had had four illegitimate sons during his first wife's life. The estate Sir William had inherited was entailed, which meant that it could descend only through the legitimate male line. Consequently in 1510 Sir William had purchased land in Leicestershire to provide Alice with an income, if he died, which would pass after her death to her eldest son. Once his wife died and he had married Alice, Sir William became involved in a dispute with his brother George and his sisters over the inheritance from their parents. He may have been putting pressure on George to agree to break the entail and let him make his eldest, illegitimate son his heir. If so, he failed. When Sir William died, Alice was left a comparatively wealthy widow, with the potential to increase her income by successfully challenging her brother-in-law over the inheritance of the Gresley estate. Within months Alice was married to Anne's father and taking legal action against George Gresley on behalf of her eldest son. The dispute eventually reached Wolsey, who in 1525 ruled as lord chancellor in favour of George Gresley, but required him to make annual payments to Alice and her sons.[2]

Although Anne may have returned to her father's house after his release, there are a number of alternative possibilities. She may have stayed with her brother and Elizabeth, keeping her sister-in-law company during her pregnancies and helping with the children who arrived in quick succession over the following years. Or she could have forged a more independent life, as a gentlewoman to Elizabeth's step-mother Eleanor, to the wife of Elizabeth's brother Henry, or to another of the ladies of Henry VIII's court. It is even possible that Wolsey took pity on her as an innocent victim of her family's lawlessness and made a place for her in his large household. That would explain her later familiarity with Thomas Cromwell, who was then in Wolsey's service.

The earliest confirmation we have that Anne Savage had arrived at the king's court was her inclusion in the list of Anne Boleyn's gentlewomen who received New Year gifts from the king in January 1532.[3] By then her father, eldest brother and the Earl of Worcester were all dead. Anne's brother John had died in 1528, aged thirty-five, leaving four young children. The following year his widow married William Brereton, a groom of the king's privy chamber and younger son of a leading Cheshire family linked by kinship ties to the Savages. Brereton had acquired some of the property forfeited by the Savages in 1516. Given the Somerset family's relationship to the king, Henry's approval would have been required for Elizabeth's marriage and he may even have encouraged the match. Brereton was a useful royal servant and by 1530 was actively engaged in the affair of the king's divorce. It may have been Brereton's influence that found his wife's sister-in-law a place in Anne Boleyn's household.

~~~

Anne Savage's future husband Thomas Berkeley was around the same age as her, having been born in 1505. His grandfather Maurice had succeeded to the barony of Berkeley in 1492. This should have been a great inheritance. The Berkeleys had held Berkeley castle since the twelfth century and had built up a considerable holding of land, predominantly in Gloucestershire and Somerset. During the fifteenth century they had been engaged in a protracted dynastic struggle over their estate, but in 1470 the rival claimant, Lord Lisle, was defeated and killed in a pitched battle. While William, lord Berkeley was obliged to pay compensation to Lisle's widow, he was not punished for his violent resolution of the feud and emerged with his rights to the disputed land confirmed. In addition he inherited through his mother a share of the extensive lands of the Mowbrays, medieval dukes of Norfolk and earls of Surrey. The other Mowbray heir was William's cousin John, lord Howard. This joint inheritance was to create a strong bond between successive generations of Howards and Berkeleys.

Lord Howard was a long-standing supporter of the Yorkist cause. He inherited his share of the Mowbray lands under Richard III and was created Duke of Norfolk. His eldest son Thomas was created Earl of Surrey. The Howards fought on the losing side at Bosworth; Norfolk was killed and after the battle Surrey was imprisoned in the Tower. When subsequently released and restored to favour, Surrey became a loyal servant of Henry VII as a military leader and a member of the privy council. By contrast their private feud had kept the Berkeleys out of the greater dynastic struggle of the rival claimants to England's throne. As a result Lord Berkeley was regarded with some suspicion by both Richard III and Henry VII. He was advanced to the rank of earl by Richard and marquess by Henry, but only at the cost of sacrificing a substantial part of the Mowbray inheritance and of ancestral Berkeley properties, including Berkeley castle. In the process he disinherited his heirs of a large part of their estate.

When William died childless in 1492, he was succeeded by his brother Maurice, Thomas's grandfather. The drastically reduced estate he inherited as a result of William's alienations was insufficient for Maurice to be recognised as a peer, entitled to be summoned to advise the king in parliament. Although he gradually managed to recover some of the alienated lands through a succession of lawsuits, Berkeley castle and a substantial part of the estate remained in the hands of the king and would descend to the king's male heirs. In 1504 Maurice leased a thirteenth-century moated and crenellated medieval manor house at Yate, with a deer park, corn mill and rabbit warren. This was to be the principal Berkeley residence in Gloucestershire for over half a century.

The disposal of much of his estate by their uncle adversely affected the marriage prospects of Maurice's younger sons. The eldest son, also Maurice, had been married aged sixteen to a slightly younger kinswoman, Katherine, the daughter of Sir William Berkeley of Stoke Gifford. The marriage settlement referred to the elder Maurice as brother and heir presumptive of the then Earl of Nottingham. It allocated manors for Katherine's support, if she were widowed, that he expected to inherit from his brother. Although the manors had been recovered by the time his son inherited the estate, this was only after a protracted legal battle. In the meantime the resources available to provide settlements for the two younger sons were limited. In 1492 James, then in his late teens or early twenties, married Susan, the young widow of William Veel of Tortworth. His brother Thomas had to wait until he was in his thirties before he married Eleanor, the daughter of Sir Marmaduke Constable of Flamborough on the east coast of Yorkshire and widow of John Ingilby of Ripley.

Both James and Thomas Berkeley married women, who were not simply widows, but were also the mothers of young sons who were the heirs to their father's estates. Under the medieval rules of feudal tenure, which still governed the possession of land in Tudor England, an orphan under the age of twenty-one became the ward of his feudal overlord. The lands he inherited from his father would be held by his lord and an allowance made for his maintenance from their income until he came of age. His marriage was also at his lord's disposal. In Tudor England such wardships were valuable commodities and wealthy fathers sought the grant of the most valuable from the king. The king's tenants in chief, such as the Berkeleys, similarly acquired and sold the wardships of their own tenants. Provided the ward lived, which was by no means certain, the guardian could expect to reap the benefit of managing the lands for years and to marry the ward to one of his own children. When a ward came of age, they could repudiate a match made for them in childhood by their guardian, if the marriage was unconsummated. If that happened, the guardian was recognised as having lost a financial benefit and could demand compensation from the former ward. The ward's mother had no rights. She had no automatic role in the upbringing of her child. The ward might be taken by the guardian into his own household at any time, and certainly after the age of seven this was very likely.

A widow was entitled to an income from the estate left by her late husband. The common law right of dower gave her a third of her husband's freehold land. Alternatively she could receive a jointure. This was income from land conveyed by the groom's family on the couple's marriage for them to hold jointly during their marriage and solely during the life of the survivor. The land was usually conveyed to trustees, who were expected to ensure a wife was not forced to agree to the sale of jointure land to settle current debts at the cost of reducing her potential income as a widow. By Henry VIII's reign jointure was far more common than dower among aristocratic families, as the increasing use of trusts by landowners made dower rights difficult to secure.

An aristocratic widow with a large income from her jointure might be able to acquire her son's wardship in her own right. So too might a mother, whose son inherited only a very small estate. Susan Veel and Eleanor Ingilby were not in either position. Both their sons were the heirs to estates that were sufficiently large to attract purchasers, who their mothers were unlikely to be able to outbid from their own resources. A second marriage to someone willing to acquire the wardship enabled a mother to bring up her son and have some say over his marriage. The potential husband got a wife with her own jointure property and the income from his step-son's estate until he came of age. Hence the incentive for Sir John Savage to pursue the Gresley inheritance for his step-son. The wardship of William Ingilby, Thomas Berkeley's step-son, was held by the Bishop of Durham. William Senhouse had been abbot of St Mary's abbey, York before he became bishop and had there worked closely with the Earl of Surrey. Sir Marmaduke Constable, another former Yorkist who after Bosworth had proved his loyalty to Henry VII, also had close ties to the Earl of Surrey. It seems likely that Surrey encouraged the marriage of Sir Marmaduke's daughter to Thomas Berkeley and the transfer of William Ingilby's wardship to them. To facilitate this his father and elder brother settled a number of manors on Thomas, including Hovingham in Ryedale. It was at Hovingham that the couple's eldest son Thomas, Anne Savage's future husband, was born in 1505. His grandfather died the following year, still not recognised as Lord Berkeley.

During Thomas's childhood the Berkeleys gradually improved their standing. His uncle Maurice was one of the twenty-six knights of the bath created at Henry VIII's coronation in 1509 and served at court as an esquire of the body to the king. His uncle James was a gentleman usher to Henry VIII and in 1510 was made constable of Berkeley castle and keeper of the park there. As constable he was entitled to live at

The Savage Marriage

the castle, except when the king required it for his own use. Meanwhile their sister Anne married William Denys of Dyrham, an esquire of the king's privy chamber. In 1513 Maurice raised and led a contingent of men in Henry VIII's invasion of France. Also in the army was Anne Savage's brother John, who was knighted after the battle of Tournai. Meanwhile, when the Scottish army took advantage of the king's absence to invade Northumberland, Thomas's father fought in the English victory at Flodden. The English army was led by the Earl of Surrey and Sir Marmaduke Constable commanded the left wing. Thomas's father was knighted in the field after the battle. Surrey himself was subsequently rewarded by being created Duke of Norfolk in recognition of his victory. Several of Anne's kinsmen fought at Flodden, where her great-uncle Sir Christopher Savage was among the English dead.

In 1514 James Berkeley died and the constableship of Berkeley castle was awarded to Thomas's father. That year the Duke of Norfolk was engaged in the negotiations for the marriage of Mary Tudor to Louis XII. When the duke escorted her to Paris, his cousin Sir Maurice Berkeley was also in the princess's train. Maurice subsequently became part of the garrison at the English enclave of Calais, rising in time to be lieutenant of the castle.

When he was about ten, Thomas's parents, his younger brother Maurice and their two sisters Mirriell and Joan moved from Yorkshire to Gloucestershire. His half-brother William remained in Yorkshire, old enough now to begin managing his own estate. Although he held the constableship of Berkeley castle, Sir Thomas did not live there. Instead Sir Maurice bought a house for them at Mangotsfield a few miles south of his own at Yate, which provided more comfortable accommodation and cost less to run than a medieval castle. With Sir Maurice based in Calais, his brother's presence helped to maintain the family's authority in Gloucestershire. Sir Maurice's wife Katherine was herself descended from a fourteenth-century Lord Berkeley and her brothers were leading members of the Gloucestershire gentry, although the family's fortunes had been adversely affected by her grandfather's support of the losing side at Bosworth. Katherine remained predominantly at Yate and managed her husband's affairs there. However, as a woman her public role was necessarily limited. Sir Thomas could actively participate in local government and maintain the family's authority in a way no woman could. Considerable amounts were spent on Yate Court and Mangotsfield, to make both houses more comfortable and sufficiently grand to reflect the family's increasing status.

When his parents left Yorkshire, Thomas started a new stage of his life away from them. His aunt and uncle having no children of their own, he was adopted as Sir Maurice's heir and his uncle took charge of his education. Thomas was to be prepared for a military life in the king's service not one as a provincial gentleman. Accordingly, he accompanied his uncle to Calais. Once there he was sent inland to St Omer, where he was placed in the care of a local priest to learn Latin and French. At St Omer the impressionable young sons of the officers at Calais were safe from the temptations of a garrison town. Temptations to which Sir Maurice himself succumbed, when he fathered his illegitimate son Humphrey by a local woman. At the same time St Omer was close enough for the boys to be brought quickly to Calais, in case of civil disturbance, the outbreak of war between the English and the French, or the arrival of a diplomatic mission. Introductions to courtiers passing through Calais on such missions might assist a young man later in making his way in the world, especially if he was able to display fluency in French during the encounter.

In 1520 Sir Maurice Berkeley was presented with an outstanding opportunity to advance his nephew, when a meeting was arranged outside Calais between Henry VIII and the French king Francis I. For this Guînes castle was converted from a satellite fortress into the headquarters of the English contingent, while a temporary palace was constructed alongside to provide accommodation fit for a king. At least two thousand workmen were employed that spring, preparing the accommodation. Hundreds of tents and pavilions were required to house the court, mountains of plates, cutlery and drinking vessels, miles of table linens. Henry VIII and Catherine of Aragon were accompanied by a suite five thousand strong, all of whom had to be housed, fed and watered for the seventeen days of the festivities. The preparations took months. They were presided over by the Earl of Worcester as lord chamberlain and Sir Maurice was one of those instructed to assist him. During the preparations and throughout the actual meeting Thomas with his now fluent French would have played his part: running errands, acting as a translator, and generally making himself useful. At the same time the tournaments, banquets, masques and dances gave him a taste of the splendour of court life. The Field of Cloth of Gold may also have marked Thomas's first encounter with Anne Boleyn, who attended as a lady in waiting to the French queen Claude and whose father Sir Thomas Boleyn, the king's ambassador to France, had also been engaged in the arrangements.

Peace with the French king did not last long and within two years Sir Maurice took part in a raid launched from Calais into France. As a further offensive was being planned in 1523, he was raised to the peerage alongside Sir William Sandys, treasurer of Calais and Sir Nicholas Vaux, lieutenant of Guînes. The grant was made as a new creation, rather than as the restoration of an ancient barony. As such, Maurice was effectively made a life peer, as he had no legitimate son and new creations did not pass to brothers or nephews. However, by the time his name was added to the list of peers for the parliament something had changed. His name was placed in the middle rather than at the bottom of the parliament roll. This indicated that the Berkeley barony had been restored to its former precedence and could descend to Maurice's male heirs.

The new Lord Berkeley never attended parliament, as he died at Calais in September 1523. While his uncle lived, Thomas's status as his adopted heir was always uncertain. If his aunt had died, his uncle could have remarried and had his own children. Young Humphrey in Calais was evidence, that this was possible. Once his uncle was dead, Thomas was in a far more certain position, although he did not come into his inheritance immediately. Yate Court and its contents passed to Maurice's widow Katherine for the remainder of her life, after which it would descend to Thomas and his male heirs. Maurice left £500 from his estate to William, the new Lord Sandys, with which he was to buy land for Humphrey, who was to remain in Calais. He also directed that his two wards, John Berkeley of Stoke Gifford and Thomas Perrot, were to marry two of his nieces.[4] Both boys, who may also have been in Calais with Maurice, were heirs to estates in Gloucestershire. As his father now succeeded as Lord Berkeley, Thomas moved from being an heir presumptive, who could be supplanted by the birth of a new heir, to the heir apparent to the barony. Although the Berkeley estate had been diminished by his great-uncle, the inheritance was still substantial. Moreover it was by now clear that the king would have no more children by Catherine of Aragon. If Henry VIII died without a male heir, Berkeley castle and its estate would revert to the family.

Although he inherited Yate Court when his aunt died two years later, Thomas did not settle in Gloucestershire. Instead his father moved to Yate, while Thomas remained in London. According to John Smyth, his main occupation over the next few years was overseeing the Berkeley's various lawsuits. It is possible that he entered one of the inns of court to complete his education. Some knowledge of the law was useful, while the inns provided a convenient base for wealthy young men keen to take advantage of all that London and Henry VIII's court had to offer. However, following legal suits was not Thomas's main reason for staying in London. He needed to be close to the king's court to make use of all the contacts his uncle had cultivated. The Berkeleys had recovered their status by service to the crown as much as by the law, and it was intended that Thomas should enhance their standing by the same means. He also maintained the family link to the Howards and in 1524 almost certainly took part in the funeral procession of the Duke of Norfolk at Thetford and was among the four hundred who sat down to the funeral feast.

The temptations of London and Henry VIII's court held obvious dangers for an eligible eighteen-year-old like Thomas Berkeley. To prevent some of them, his family decided to find him a wife before he found an unsuitable one for himself. Accordingly, his father began negotiations with the new Duke of Norfolk for a marriage between Thomas and Katherine, one of the duke's daughters by his second wife Elizabeth Stafford. Katherine's mother was one of the daughters of Edward, duke of Buckingham, who had been the premier peer and richest of the king's subjects. Buckingham had been a towering figure in Gloucestershire, where he held Thornbury castle, until in 1521 he was arrested, convicted of having 'imagined and compassed' the king's death and executed.[5] Through her Stafford mother the proposed bride was descended from Edward III. The negotiations proceeded to the point where a settlement was drawn up and the first part of the dowry was paid, but the marriage never took place. Why this was is not clear. John Smyth speculated that Katherine died, or that the couple were deemed to be too closely related, or that they disliked each other when they eventually met. However, we know

The Savage Marriage

that Katherine lived to marry the Earl of Derby in 1529, dying of the plague a few months later, while obtaining a dispensation to deal with the relationship would have been straightforward, and Tudor parents were not renowned for taking the likes and dislikes of their children into account when arranging their marriages. Indeed Katherine's mother had been forced to marry Howard against her will by her father and their unhappy marriage eventually resulted in a complete separation. It is possible that Katherine's age was the problem, as the marriage could not happen until she was twelve. Not only might the temptations of London and the court prove too much for Thomas in the interim, but his father wanted to get his hands on the dowry quickly to finance the marriages of his own two daughters

Whatever the reason an alternative match was quickly arranged between Thomas and Katherine's cousin, Mary Hastings. Mary was the daughter of George, lord Hastings, a close friend of the king and member of the royal household. Her mother Anne was the sister of the executed Duke of Buckingham. Lord Hastings had met Thomas while in attendance on the king at the Field of Cloth of Gold and later when he was on campaign in France. By midsummer 1527 Thomas and both his sisters were married. Mirriell married Robert, the eldest son of Sir George Throckmorton of Coughton, Warwickshire, while Joan married Nicholas, eldest son of Sir Anthony Poyntz of Iron Acton. Thomas would have met both Sir George Throckmorton and Sir Anthony Poyntz during his time in France. Sir George had been there in attendance on his father-in-law Sir Nicholas Vaux, who as the lieutenant of Guînes had worked closely with Maurice Berkeley. Sir Anthony Poyntz had commanded a ship during the French war and subsequently passed through Calais on an embassy to the French king, as well as being present at the Field of Cloth of Gold. Thomas and his sisters were part of a tightly knit circle dominated by the Duke of Norfolk and linked by ties of marriage.

As these marriages were being arranged, Thomas's mother Eleanor died. The following year his father remarried. John Smyth would in relation to a later Berkeley marriage rehearse the arguments against the 'amorous humour' that led old men to marry, when there was no prospect of producing children.[6] In this case it was a financially advantageous match, of which Smyth approved. Lord Berkeley's new wife was Cicely, the widow of Richard Rowdon, a wealthy merchant and alderman of Gloucester. Her brother John Arnold was a lawyer and steward to Gloucester Abbey. John Arnold held the manor of Highnam outside Gloucester, where Lord Berkeley and his new bride stayed after their wedding. By her first marriage Cicely had two daughters, Frances and Katherine, co-heiresses of both their father and his brother. In the autumn of 1527 Lord Berkeley negotiated with John Arnold not only the terms of his own marriage to their mother, but that of the elder daughter Frances to his younger son Maurice. Such reciprocal marriages were not uncommon in Tudor England. Through his marriage Maurice acquired Richard Rowdon's former house in the centre of Gloucester and other property, including a large tavern.[7] The pattern established by the previous generation was set to continue. Thomas was in attendance on the Duke of Norfolk, predominantly following the court as it moved between the various royal houses along the Thames from Greenwich to Windsor and further afield during the summer progress. His brother lived at Mangotsfield and assisted his father in maintaining the Berkeley influence in Gloucestershire. His house in Gloucester provided a convenient base, when he needed to visit the town for the assizes and other business. Meanwhile John Arnold, who became the steward of Lord Berkeley's Gloucestershire manors, was a useful ally.

Following their marriage Thomas and Mary were given an allowance of £100 by his father, although he apparently retained a third of this for three years in order to fund repairs to Mangotsfield. While this was a sufficient income for a country gentleman, it would not sustain a couple at court. As she was still young, it is likely that Mary stayed with her family at their house in Stoke Poges, Buckinghamshire, where Thomas would have been able to visit her regularly.

~~~

Attending Norfolk to the king's court gave Thomas many opportunities to become acquainted with the queen's ladies in waiting. Among them was the duke's niece Anne Boleyn, with whom Thomas would have been able to chat in French, although the idioms he had learnt among the soldiers at Calais were probably less refined than those common among Queen Claude's ladies. Thomas was well-placed to observe Anne's rise and the stuttering progress of the king's divorce. He may well have been in the party that accompanied the

The Savage Marriage

dukes of Norfolk and Suffolk in the autumn of 1529 to relieve Cardinal Wolsey of the great seal, the symbol of his office as lord chancellor. A few weeks later Thomas's father-in-law received his patent as Earl of Huntingdon, in recognition of his support over the divorce. The following year Thomas's own father was among those peers, who signed a petition urging the pope to grant the king a divorce. Thomas was firmly within the camp that supported the king's wish to divorce Catherine of Aragon and marry Anne Boleyn.

After Wolsey's fall Norfolk took over the general administration of the household of Henry's illegitimate son, the duke of Richmond. Norfolk's own son Henry, earl of Surrey became Richmond's companion and the two became close friends, spending much of the next six years in each other's company. In 1529 the Spanish ambassador reported a rumour that Anne Boleyn was encouraging Henry to consent to a marriage between Surrey and Princess Mary. If there was any substance to this rumour, it came to nothing. However, the king was persuaded to agree that Norfolk's daughter Mary should marry Richmond. In the spring of 1532 Surrey married Frances de Vere, daughter of the Earl of Oxford and a maid of honour to Princess Mary. As plans were then being made for Richmond and Surrey to stay at the French court, it seems Norfolk wanted to avoid Surrey finding himself an unsuitable bride in France. Richmond's marriage to Mary Howard took place in November 1533, once they were both of age.

In the late summer of 1532 preparations were underway for a meeting between Henry VIII and Francis I at Boulogne and Calais. This was an opportunity for Anne Boleyn to be presented on the European stage as Henry's intended bride. Since Francis had previously known Anne as one of his wife's ladies in waiting, it was essential that her status should be formally enhanced before they met again. Accordingly, on 1 September Anne Boleyn was created Marchioness of Pembroke in a magnificent ceremony at Windsor castle. Anne was conducted by the countesses of Rutland and Derby into the presence of the king, who was flanked by the dukes of Norfolk and Suffolk. The crimson mantle and gold coronet of a marquess were carried by Norfolk's daughter Mary. The French ambassador was a guest of honour. After a solemn high mass in St George's chapel, conducted by the Bishop of Winchester, there was a great banquet attended by most of the court. Thomas Berkeley would have been there in attendance on Norfolk and Anne Savage as a member of Anne Boleyn's household. Elizabeth Holland, Norfolk's mistress, was also there in attendance on Anne Boleyn. There were, however, some notable exceptions. Henry's sister Mary, duchess of Suffolk had refused to take part in the ceremony, as had Norfolk's estranged wife.

On 11 October Henry and Anne crossed to France with a considerable company of courtiers. Thomas with his useful knowledge of French and of Calais accompanied Norfolk, while his brother-in-law Nicholas Poyntz was in the king's train. Anne Savage was one of the twenty ladies in attendance on Anne. Thomas's wife may have gone as well, but it is more likely that she was left at home in Stoke Poges. The meeting was not as lavish and grand as the Field of Cloth of Gold, but it achieved its purpose of announcing Anne's status as Henry's intended wife. The return of the royal party was delayed by bad weather in the Channel. It is widely believed that it was during their enforced extended stay in Calais, that Henry VIII and Anne Boleyn finally consummated their relationship. Other flirtations may also have developed into something more, among the young courtiers away from their usual routines and kept indoors by the weather. It is probable that Thomas Berkeley and Anne Savage were among those getting better acquainted.

Having been unwell for more than a year, in January 1533 Thomas's father lay dying at Mangotsfield. Summoned to his death bed alongside his family were two local abbots, a prior, a dean and other local clergy. It is not clear at what point in the proceedings Thomas arrived, but he was apparently there when his father died on 22 January. Thomas, as the new Lord Berkeley, remained in Gloucestershire for the funeral masses in the church at Mangotsfield and the elaborate procession when his father's corpse was carried the six miles to Bristol to lay alongside his first wife in St Augustine's abbey. It was only after the funeral, that the formal transfer of the lordship of Berkeley from his father to Thomas was deemed to have taken place. Consequently Thomas was not at court when the clandestine marriage of Henry VIII and Anne Boleyn took place.

Although the estate that Thomas inherited from his father in 1533 had been depleted by his great-uncle, he received considerable landholdings in Gloucestershire, across the Midlands and in Sussex. There was also property in Ireland and Calais. His brother Maurice received a life interest in Mangotsfield, the property that had originally been acquired by their uncle to provide a Gloucestershire base for his own younger brother. Seven manors had been allocated to provide their step-mother Cicely with her jointure. Thomas was made constable of Berkeley castle by the king six weeks after his father's death. The building work that his uncle and father had undertaken at Yate and Mangotsfield, the cost of dowries for his two sisters and other extraordinary expenses had left an accumulation of debts, to which were added those Thomas had himself run up on his own account. Pursuing royal favour at court, where gambling was a popular pursuit, tended to be an expensive affair. Norfolk may have paid the tailor to ensure he was suitably dressed, but gambling debts were another matter. Such debts were commonplace and, provided a man's income was sufficient, not a problem. John Smyth described Thomas's father, who had been 'sparingly bred in youth', as having retained his frugal habits after inheriting the title. Despite this he included in his will compensation to his daughter-in-law Frances for a gold chain inherited from her father, which he had sold 'at my greate need'. He also owed his other step-daughter £50, due from the wills of her uncle and father.[8] With his exposure to the seductive attractions of Henry VIII's court, Thomas was unlikely to adopt an economical, provincial lifestyle. Retiring to Yate would prevent him from taking advantage of the connections he had been cultivating. Moreover, as a member of the House of Lords he would now be called upon to play an active, if junior, role in the legal settlement of the consequences of the king's divorce. So once his father's funeral rites were completed, it was inevitable that Thomas would return to court.

Maurice's life interest in Mangotsfield had been agreed at the time of his marriage, but Thomas now disputed this. Since the lands their father had left Maurice were not specified in the will itself, there was room for dispute. The appointment of his step-mother Cicely and her brother John Arnold as executors no doubt contributed to Thomas's feeling, that he was being cheated. He claimed, that he had contributed towards the repairs to Mangotsfield from his allowance and accepted the use of materials from his own house at Yate, on the understanding that he would inherit the property unencumbered. He also disputed whether some of what Maurice claimed formed part of the Mangotsfield property at all. His insistence on taking legal action against Maurice put Thomas at odds with Cicely, both as executrix and Maurice's mother-in-law, and with his brother-in-law Nicholas Poyntz.

Within weeks of Thomas becoming Lord Berkeley, his wife Mary died. The cause of her death is unrecorded and we do not know whether it was sudden or if she had been ill for some time. There was no fixed period of mourning and, while widows were expected to wait long enough to ensure that there would be no uncertainty about a child's parentage, no such consideration prevented a man from remarrying quickly. When Lord William Howard, Norfolk's younger brother, found himself a childless widower in 1535, he hastily remarried and his son was born the following year. The lack of an heir gave Thomas a strong incentive to remarry speedily, but the arrangement of an aristocratic marriage usually involved complex financial arrangements, that took time to arrange. When Norfolk had lost his first wife in 1511, it took almost two years to arrange his marriage to Elizabeth Stafford, despite him being nearly forty and with no son to succeed him. It may in part have been the speed with which Thomas married Anne Savage after Mary's death which gave rise to the rumour that the king and his new queen 'contrived' the marriage as a reward for her loyalty and discretion over their own wedding.[9]

There may have been a strong incentive for Thomas and Anne not to delay their marriage in the spring of 1533. John Smyth dated the marriage to sometime in April, based on the birth of their first child no later than January 1534. However, when Anne gave birth is not recorded and it may have been towards the end of 1533. After giving birth, Anne spent the traditional period of seclusion in her chamber, before the mass that marked her reintroduction to society. She later told her son, born at the end of the following November, that he was conceived the night after this churching ceremony. Either Anne was unusually fecund, or dates were quietly adjusted to create the impression that both her children were conceived within the marriage. It seems more likely that the wedding happened in May than April. It was in May that Anne's marriage settlement was concluded and Thomas came to an agreement with Cicely to exchange a number of

The Savage Marriage

the manors she held for an annuity. The trustees for Anne's settlement were the king's secretary Thomas Cromwell and her husband's former father-in-law, the Earl of Huntingdon with his son Francis, lord Hastings. On 20 May 1533 Cromwell was made steward of the Gloucestershire manors covered by the settlement and the Earl of Huntingdon and his son of those in Leicestershire.

It is therefore very likely that Anne was already pregnant at the time of her marriage and may even have conceived like her mistress during the enforced extension to their stay in Calais. Tudor pregnancies were not confirmed until the child began to stir in the womb at around four months. So Anne may have realised she was pregnant around the same time as Mary died and Thomas became free to marry her. Anne Boleyn, anxious to avoid scandal within her household at this crucial juncture, may well have encouraged the match, regardless of whether Anne Savage had been a witness to her own wedding. Cromwell's involvement suggests the king and queen approved of the match. Anne's dowry was 500 marks (about £333). The source of the money is not clear, but it was not uncommon for queens to provide dowries for impoverished ladies in waiting. The amount was less than that provided for Thomas's two sisters on their marriages and again helps to explain the surprise that was felt over their marriage and the search for an explanation.

His marriage to Anne Savage may also mark Thomas's growing independence from Norfolk, whose relationship with his niece had become increasingly strained during the course of the king's divorce proceedings. In May 1533 Norfolk was sent to France on a fruitless embassy that effectively kept him away from Anne Boleyn's coronation.

On Thursday 29 May 1533 Thomas and Anne were with the court at Greenwich, when a great flotilla of barges carrying London's civic dignitaries arrived to accompany Anne Boleyn to the Tower, where by tradition monarchs spent the days immediately before their coronation. As a baroness Anne may have travelled in the first sumptuously decorated barge with Anne Boleyn and the principal ladies of the court, rather than in the second barge with the remainder of her women. Thomas would have been in another barge among the throng of courtiers. By tradition the king would remain unseen during the queen's coronation, so Henry travelled separately to the Tower and greeted his wife in private after her formal entrance.

The royal party spent forty-eight hours at the Tower, where the royal apartments had been reconstructed for the occasion. For Thomas, his former brother-in-law Francis Hastings, Alice Savage's former brother-in-law George Gresley and fifteen other courtiers, predominantly Boleyn and Howard supporters, the period from Friday dinner until Saturday morning was taken up with the ceremonies for making them knights of the bath, including an overnight vigil in the White Tower. Late on Saturday afternoon a grand procession conducted Anne Boleyn from the Tower through the city to Westminster. Thomas rode with his fellow knights of the bath ahead of the queen, while Anne was among the ladies in crimson velvet following immediately behind. On Whit Sunday Thomas donned the parliament robes he had inherited from his father and with his fellow peers preceded the queen into Westminster Abbey for her coronation. Anne was among the host of ladies and gentlewomen in scarlet, who followed Anne Boleyn into the abbey. There Anne Boleyn was crowned queen by the Archbishop of Canterbury during a lengthy service, while the king watched from behind a lattice. The host then processed back to Westminster Hall for the coronation feast. The queen sat in lonely but splendid isolation at a table shared by only the archbishop, seated at one end. Norfolk's half-sister, the dowager Countess of Oxford, and the Countess of Worcester, sister-in-law to Elizabeth Brereton (formerly Savage), stood beside the queen. From time to time they held up a cloth to conceal her from the other diners, so she could spit unseen. During the feast Anne's place at table was determined by her husband's precedence in the peerage. Thomas and the other new knights of the bath had the ceremonial duty of carrying in the first course of dishes for the queen. The feast concluded the formal ceremonies, but the next day there were jousts, balls and a banquet held in the queen's apartments, all of which Thomas and Anne would have attended as participants or spectators.

After the coronation Anne and Thomas went to stay at Berkeley castle, formally acknowledging his appointment as constable. From there Anne wrote to Cromwell about a grant of part of the estate, which, if allowed by the king, would be deleterious to her and her husband's interests. Her letters to the king's secretary reveal a confident woman, determined to defend her and her husband's interests.[10] The couple's whereabouts over the next few months are unknown, but Thomas's challenging of his father's will would have required consultations with his legal advisors and appearance at the Westminster law courts. At some point in the following winter Anne gave birth to a daughter, who they named Elizabeth. If this indeed happened as late as January, it is likely that the birth occurred in London, as in 1534 Thomas attended all the sessions of the House of Lords from when it met on 15 January until 4 February. Thereafter his attendance became intermittent and in March he was present for just three sessions in the middle of the month.

Lord Berkeley's absence from parliament in March 1534 was in part due to his being occupied elsewhere. At the beginning of the month news of the death of the abbot of Croxton arrived in London. The Premonstratensian abbey of Croxton, which lay to the north-east of Melton Mowbray in Leicestershire close to the border with Lincolnshire, had been endowed by one of Thomas's ancestors. Thomas consequently claimed the right as patron to present his own candidate as abbot. The monks protested to Cromwell that they had traditionally elected their abbots and intended to do so again, but agreed to delay the election until the end of April. As the day for the election drew near, Thomas sent two of his armed retainers to take control of the abbey from the monks. Two days later Thomas himself arrived with his cousin James Berkeley and some forty armed men. He claimed that he had been offered 500 marks for the appointment, presumably by Robert Derby for whom a nomination survives in the Berkeley archive.[11] Thomas offered to allow the election to go ahead in return for a payment of £500. At this point John Maxey, the abbot of Welbeck in Nottinghamshire, intervened. He held a commission from the king as visitor for the English Premonstratensian houses. The stand off, between the monks and the armed men preventing them from entering the chapterhouse to hold their election, was eventually resolved by an immediate payment of £160 to Thomas and the promise of a further £160 at a later date. The election went ahead and the monks chose their own candidate as abbot.[12] Thomas's interference in the election of the new abbot may have been politically motivated and encouraged by Cromwell, as a way of unsettling the monks and dissuading them from opposing the new church settlement. Around the same time William Brereton used similar tactics to extort a bond from the incoming abbot of the Cistercian abbey of Vale Royal, Cheshire. The events at Croxall certainly demonstrate that Anne's husband was as prepared to use force of arms, intimidation and extortion to serve his own interests as ever her father or brother had been.

Later that spring Thomas and Anne spent some time at Yate, but a wish to cultivate the continuation of royal favour dictated that they should not remain in the country. Leaving Elizabeth with a wet nurse in Gloucestershire, they returned to London in early July. There Thomas joined twenty of his fellow peers in the trial of Lord Dacre, the only peer found innocent of treason during Henry VIII's reign. The Berkeleys had agreed to lease a house at Stone near Dartford in Kent from the widow of Sir John Wiltshire, who had been comptroller of Calais. Sir John's daughter Bridget had been in the retinue of Catherine of Aragon at the Field of Cloth of Gold and was later close to Anne Boleyn. Stone provided a useful stopping place for diplomats and others on journeys between the court and France. Henry and Anne Boleyn had stayed there overnight on their return from Calais in November 1532. As Bridget died some time in 1534, Thomas presumably agreed the lease with Lady Wiltshire after her daughter's death, ensuring that diplomats could continue to receive appropriate hospitality on their journeys from someone familiar with Calais. Stone also provided easy communication by river to the royal palaces on the Thames, so Anne and Thomas would be able to maintain their profile at court. Following the Dacre trial, they established themselves at Stone with six male attendants and two gentlewomen to serve Anne. By then Anne knew she was pregnant with their second child.

Two months later on 19 September Thomas died at Stone after a short illness. He had made no will. His death was later ascribed by family tradition to a surfeit of cherries. Anne was left in an uncertain position. If the child she was carrying was a boy, he would inherit his father's title. If it was a girl, Anne and her children would have only her jointure. The title, Yate Court, and the Berkeley estate would pass to his brother as the heir male. As Thomas had been at odds with Maurice for the previous eighteen months, this did not augur well for Anne's future. With Cromwell and the Hastings as her trustees Anne's jointure was secure, but it would not provide the glittering future she had envisaged.

2 A Widow and Her Children

Anne left Stone after Thomas's funeral and travelled to Caludon near Coventry, one of the manors included in her jointure. The Berkeleys had acquired a medieval castle there as part of the Mowbray estate, but that was in poor repair and more commodious accommodation was available in an adjoining manor house. Although Caludon was part of Anne's jointure, she stayed there as the guest of Thomas Try, who had leased the manor from Thomas's grandmother. Despite being heavily pregnant, in early November Anne travelled to Gloucestershire for her lying in. If she was carrying a son, it was important that no-one would be able to claim there was anything untoward about his entry into the world. At Yate on 26 November she gave birth to a son. The baby was named Henry, in honour of the king who agreed to stand as godfather.

From the moment of his birth Henry was the king's ward. If Anne was to play a role in Henry's upbringing, it was important that his wardship should either be retained by the king or granted to someone sympathetic to her. In the event the king granted the wardship to Robert Radcliffe, earl of Sussex, who had supported him over the divorce and played an important ceremonial role at Anne Boleyn's coronation. He was linked by his marriages to both the Staffords and the Hastings, while his son had married Norfolk's half-sister. Sussex assigned the wardship to Anne, presumably in exchange for a suitable monetary reward or favourable grant of land or stewardship. Anne thus secured the custody of her two children and the right to manage their upbringing. She was reported as being very tender-hearted towards them and hardly able to let them out of her sight. As a widow in control of her son's lands, she had an unusual degree of autonomy for a Tudor woman. Such a degree of independence would be lost, if she remarried. Her husband would expect and be expected to make decisions on behalf of her and her children.

John Smyth, who described Anne as 'a lady of masculine spirit, over-powerfull with her husband', put most of the blame for the dispute over Mangotsfield on her.[1] This is unfair, as Thomas initiated and actively prosecuted the case until his death. He also demonstrated over his dealings with the monks of Croxton that he was willing to use force to obtain his ends. Tudor legal disputes over land were rarely conducted only in court. Direct action was also used to ensure that the opposition did not enjoy quiet possession of disputed property. Hedges and fences would be torn up, weirs broken and hayricks burnt. Before Thomas died, the dispute over Mangotsfield had escalated to this level. In June 1534 a riotous party of over thirty of his supporters damaged the manor's mill pond, which was then in Maurice's possession, and poached the fish. For this the ringleader James Berkeley of Bradley near Wotton-under-Edge and others were fined. This was the cousin, who had accompanied Thomas to Croxton and was clearly one of his closest associates. After Thomas's death Anne retained James as steward of a number of her manors. She also continued to prosecute the legal case against Maurice's possession of Mangotsfield. There is no sign that the blighting of her adolescence by violent local feuding made her at all reluctant to become engaged in the dispute. She also attempted to get the abbot of Croxton to pay the bond he had given Thomas, which he refused on the grounds that he had been falsely imprisoned and forced to sign the bond under duress. Her sister-in-law Elizabeth Brereton was later involved in similar legal proceedings over the bond her husband had extorted from the abbot of Vale Royal.

As a woman Anne was debarred from some forms of direct action, but her sex could be an advantage when appealing for support. In the summer of 1535 the powerful resources on which Anne could draw were brought to the attention of her neighbours, when the king and queen visited Gloucestershire on their summer progress. In August the royal couple spent a week at Berkeley castle followed by a week at Thornbury. In preparation for their stay Thomas Cromwell in conjunction with his nephew Richard was made constable of Berkeley castle. As the accommodation at the castles was insufficient for the whole court, Anne was in a position to offer comfortable lodgings at Yate to some of her former colleagues. This was hospitality offered *in abstentia*, as Anne was at Caludon on the day the royal party arrived at Berkeley.[2] In her dispute with Maurice Berkeley all the advantage of powerful contacts did not lie with Anne. From Thornbury the royal party moved onto Acton Court, where Nicholas Poyntz had added a new wing to his house to accommodate them. It is likely that Poyntz received his knighthood as the culmination of this visit.

In May 1536 two of Anne's most important contacts at court were swept away, as Henry VIII divested himself of his second wife more quickly and ruthlessly than he had his first. Anne Boleyn was arrested, accused of adultery and treason. Part of the evidence collected against the queen were the alleged deathbed remarks of Bridget Wiltshire. Among those accused of being the queen's lovers was William Brereton. Although Brereton and his co-accused had almost certainly not slept with the queen, they were all found guilty and executed. The queen, whose real crime was failing to give Henry a male heir, followed her supposed lovers to the Tower. Once convicted, she was executed by a swordsman brought from Calais for the purpose. Lady Berkeley's sister-in-law Elizabeth was a widow once again and this time her husband's goods were forfeit as a result of his conviction for treason. Although the rights of her Savage children were protected, the future was bleak for her two sons by Brereton.

Unlike Anne Boleyn's other supposed lovers, Brereton was not a court gallant who engaged in the sort of badinage with the queen that was open to malign misinterpretation. He was very much made from the same mould as Lady Berkeley's father, brother and husband. As a landowner and officeholder he was not averse to using violence and intimidation to obtain legal or political advantage. As steward for the Duke of Richmond in North Wales Brereton had presented an obstacle to Cromwell's attempts to reform the administration of the principality. In 1534 he had used his influence to block Cromwell's attempts to save a local gentleman from the gallows. While not all of his actions were as blatant as in this case, his acceptance of bribes and his disregard for the authority of the Council of Wales made him a nuisance. When the opportunity arose, Cromwell engineered his downfall alongside Anne Boleyn.

Having previously distanced himself from his niece, Norfolk was not brought down by her fall. His influence, however, waned as that of Cromwell increased and in July 1536 he received further blows. Firstly, the king discovered that Norfolk's half-brother Lord Thomas Howard had contracted a secret engagement with Lady Margaret Douglas, the daughter of the king's sister Margaret Tudor by her second marriage. As both Henry's daughters had been declared illegitimate, this clandestine marriage to his niece was interpreted by Henry as evidence of Howard designs on the throne. Incandescent with rage, he sent both parties to the Tower. The king was particularly incensed, as his only male heir was at the time lying ill in St James's palace. A few days later the Duke of Richmond died. As Richmond and Mary Howard had never co-habited, her status as his widow was uncertain. Arguments between the king and her father went on for years, leaving Mary largely dependent on Norfolk.

The demise of her former mistress and of William Brereton did not encourage Lady Berkeley to rein in her combative spirit and keep a low profile. In November 1536 John Barlow, dean of Westbury-on-Trym wrote to Cromwell complaining of her conduct. When passing through Yate at Michaelmas on his way to attend the quarter sessions in Gloucester, Barlow had come across fourteen 'evil-disposed' people playing tennis instead of attending church.[3] Although the offenders ran off at his approach, he took some names and intended to present them at the sessions. When the time came he found that the jury included a high proportion of Anne's servants and decided to hold the matter over to the assizes, where he stood more chance of getting a conviction. Furious over the matter, Anne railed at the dean, wished the men had beaten him, and threatened to sit on his skirts. The previous year Barlow and Sir Nicholas Poyntz had tried to seize a priest called William Norton for owning forbidden books, supportive of the pope. Anne now caused her supporters to indict Barlow for trespass over the affair. Barlow and Anne knew each other well, having both been members of Anne Boleyn's household. How far the dispute was simply a clash between fervent reformers and the more religiously conservative Anne is unclear, because of this former association and Poyntz's support for Maurice Berkeley in the dispute over Mangotsfield.

Anne and her son were a thorn in Maurice Berkeley's side and he too was not above the use of violence and intimidation. He and his supporters began to break into her park at Yate during the night to poach the deer. Eventually Anne brought a case in Star Chamber, a court operating under the control of the king and his council which could dispense a rapid and decisive form of justice. It was alleged that Maurice and his cronies had planned to set alight a store of hay that was close to the house, hoping the flames would spread and that Anne and her son would die in the ensuing blaze. Their plans were conveniently overheard by another group of poachers, who were hiding behind the haystack. Maurice was allegedly deterred from carrying out his plan, when he spotted this second group of poachers making a speedy getaway. The whole episode seems contrived. It may have been concocted to justify the resort to Star Chamber, which required some form of riot to have occurred. However contrived, the account demonstrates the animosity between the parties and their supporters. The Star Chamber case did not resolve the matter and the attacks on property and the vexatious litigation continued. Anne eventually used her influence to acquire a special commission from the king to hear the case against her brother-in-law and had herself made one of the commissioners. Her participation in this hearing at Gloucester led to a local belief that she had been appointed a justice of the peace. The dissension between Anne and her brother-in-law was resolved only by the latter's death around 1547, when ownership of Mangotsfield reverted to Anne's son.

It was widely assumed that a widow would and should be eager to remarry, although Anne seems to have had no inclination in this direction. In 1537 she received a visit from Edward Sutton, the teenage son of John, lord Dudley. The boy was presumably travelling through Gloucestershire on his way from the Midlands, where his parents lived, to visit some of his relatives in the South West. The Suttons were in dire financial straits. Edward's father had inherited the title in 1532 and immediately started selling off land to settle his debts. The family was largely dependent on the hospitality of their wealthier relatives to maintain an aristocratic lifestyle. Anne was well-acquainted with the Suttons, as they belonged to the same convoluted network of family ties as the Savages and the Somersets. Eleanor, the second wife of Charles, earl of Worcester and step-mother to Anne's sister-in-law Elizabeth, was Edward's aunt. Another aunt had married Sir George Gresley, brother-in-law to Anne's own step-mother Alice. Edward was clearly treated kindly by Anne, who showed him to his chamber herself and sent her gentlewomen to entertain him. Quite how she showed him 'she would suffer me to lie in her lap' is unclear, but it is unlikely that she took him seriously as a potential suitor. He was less than half her age with no position, title or other obvious attraction. She was perhaps amused by and prepared to indulge a young man's first attempts at courtly flirtation.[4]

While the Suttons were comparatively poor and unimportant,

Wives of the Berkeleys

Edward's mother was the daughter of the first Marquess of Dorset and her nephew Henry, the third marquess, had recently married the king's niece Frances, daughter of the Duke and Duchess of Suffolk. Cecily, lady Dudley was at that time relying on the hospitality of the prioress of Nuneaton and saw the marriage of her son to a wealthy widow as an obvious and immediate solution to her family's ills. She petitioned the king and Cromwell for their support in promoting a match between Edward and Anne. As Anne was the widow of one of the king's tenants in chief, theoretically he could compel her to marry. Shortly before Christmas Edward arrived once more, armed with letters from the king and Cromwell recommending his suit to Anne. She seems to have treated him quite gently, rejecting his offer on the grounds that she was not minded to marry anyone. He did not suffer one of her outbursts and, while his welcome was cooler than before, he went away thinking that a command from the king would persuade her to accept him. In her responses to the king and Cromwell, however, Anne made it clear that she was not yet ready to consider any marriage. Moreover, even were she ready to marry, Edward Sutton would not suit her. Given that Edward was so much younger than Anne and lacked either the fortune or higher status to tempt her into marriage, it is unlikely that either Henry or Cromwell expected anything else. They probably thought Edward was lucky not to be sent away with a flea in his ear. No further attempts seem to have been made to persuade Anne to abandon her widowed state.[5]

As a widow Anne leased a house on St Augustine's Green, Bristol in addition to Yate Court. There she was a close neighbour of Cicely, her husband's step-mother who had retired to Bristol some years before. Presumably the convenience of the location just across the Frome from the bustle of the city made up for any awkwardness with the neighbours. Although the house was a short stone's throw away from one of Bristol's two grammar schools, her son Henry was not enrolled as a pupil. Both Anne's children would later complain of their want of education.

It may have been an eagerness to escape the proximity of her in-laws that made Caludon in Warwickshire particularly attractive to Anne as an alternative place to live. When her steward Thomas Try died in 1545, Anne tried to take possession of the manor house immediately. Try's widow objected that she had the right to hold it for a further twelve years. A Chancery case ensued. During this Try's illegitimate son Gerard, a soldier at Boulogne, gave evidence for the Berkeleys. He later alleged that he was promised an annuity of £40 by Anne in return for his evidence, but never received it. Alongside the legal case there were also similar riotous entries onto the property as in the Mangotsfield dispute, before Anne gained possession two years later. She subsequently seized a house and land that Try had bought at Binley near Caludon. Gerard Try attempted to regain possession of this property, which he had inherited from his father, but found himself in an unequal battle. Thomas Goodrich, bishop of Ely and lord chancellor, advised him to come to an agreement with Anne rather than seeking redress at law. As Goodrich has been a royal chaplain involved in Henry VIII's divorce from Catherine of Aragon and close to the Boleyns, he may have had personal experience of Anne's tenacity. Try's personal approaches to Anne achieved nothing. When he persisted in the early years of Mary I's reign, she threatened him with being burnt as a heretic. This was an ominous threat to make to the protestant Try, who retreated abroad until the following reign. The matter was only settled after Anne's death, when her son agreed to pay Try, by then a poor curate, an annuity in return for the disputed property.

One of the attractions of Caludon for Anne throughout her widowhood was its proximity to the road from London to Cheshire, which passed through Coventry. This made it a convenient place for her kinsmen to break their journeys to and from the capital. When travelling between Bristol or Yate and Caludon, Anne was able to break her own journey with Christopher Savage, the son of her great-uncle who had died at Flodden. This branch of the Savage family had established themselves in the area of southern Worcestershire that Anne had known well as a child, acquiring the manor of Elmley Castle in 1544. One of the advantages that Anne enjoyed as a widow was being able to appoint clergymen to vacant livings, where the Berkeleys held the patronage. In 1558 she appointed Christopher Savage's younger son George as rector of Seagrave, Leicestershire. He also became rector of Saintbury, where his brother John lived, and archdeacon of Gloucestershire. Four years later she appointed Richard Smyth to Hoby, another Leicestershire parish controlled by the Berkeleys. Richard Smyth was the uncle of John Smyth, who began his education in the church school at Hoby and would later become the historian of the Berkeley family.

~~~

During the latter years of Henry VIII's reign Norfolk's fortunes had waxed and waned. The failure of Henry's marriage to Anne of Cleves had enabled the duke, as the leader of a conservative, catholic faction at court, to engineer the overthrow of Thomas Cromwell. Then he saw a second niece, Katherine Howard, become queen. Once again triumph turned to disaster, when Katherine was found to have been sexually experienced before her marriage and unfaithful after. Still Norfolk survived. Then in December 1546 it seemed his luck had finally run out. He and his son Surrey were arrested and found themselves in the Tower accused of treason. At that time there was much jockeying for position, as members of the king's council sought the power that would result from the creation on his death of a regency to rule on behalf of his infant son. The faction opposing the Howards was led by the young prince's Seymour uncles. Surrey was inordinately proud of his noble blood and regarded the Seymours as upstarts. He had made his feelings plain, by opposing a proposed marriage of his sister Mary, the widowed duchess of Richmond to Thomas Seymour. This effectively scuppered his father's attempt to make an alliance with the Seymours. The central pillar of the case against Surrey at his trial was that he had changed his coat of arms, adopting those of his executed grandfather, the Duke of Buckingham. This heraldic pretension served to remind his peers that through his mother Surrey was directly descended from Edward III. He may have wanted to draw attention to his royal lineage as a reason for him to be appointed regent. He may have had higher ambitions, thinking that should the young prince die he would be a better candidate for the throne than either of Henry VIII's daughters. In the febrile atmosphere that surrounded the paranoid and ailing king, it was not difficult for Surrey's opponents to bring a charge of treason, suggesting that the earl might seek to seize the throne on Henry's death.

When Surrey was arrested in London, he had two sons and three daughters aged between ten and three. They were then living at the palatial family house at Kenninghall in Norfolk with their heavily pregnant mother. The red-brick house, which Norfolk had built in the years immediately after he became duke, was set in seven hundred acres of deer park. Its seventy rooms set around two courts provided accommodation for the duke, his mistress Elizabeth Holland, each of his children and their families, as well as a host of household officials, servants and guests. (Norfolk's estranged wife had a separate household in Hertfordshire.) Kenninghall offered far more comfortable lodgings than the family's ancestral base at Framlingham castle across the border in Suffolk. Following Surrey's arrest, the Duchess of Richmond and Elizabeth Holland were sent to London for questioning. The children and their mother remained at Kenninghall, while the household officers and servants were questioned and the contents of the house inventoried. The atmosphere of fear, distress and upheaval that prevailed before they were wrenched from their familiar environment must have made a deep impression on the older children.

Both Surrey and his father were convicted of treason. Surrey was beheaded in January 1547. Norfolk was awaiting his own execution, when the king himself died at the end of that month. Although Norfolk's death warrant had been signed, the regency council did not carry it out. While he remained a prisoner in the Tower, Norfolk was no threat to them. Prisoners in the Tower were required to find their own daily living costs and were attended by their own servants. It was not a luxurious life, but Norfolk was allowed some home comforts as befitted his rank. Gradually the strictness of his captivity was reduced, allowing Norfolk to take exercise in the gardens of his prison. After two years his estranged wife and his daughter were allowed to visit him, although the state of his relationship with both of them means that may not have been much comfort. Presumably he took more pleasure in seeing his younger son a few months later.

Once Surrey was executed, his children's situation became more settled. Initially, his elder son Thomas was placed with Sir John Williams, the treasurer of the Court of Augmentations, and sent to live at Ricote, near Thame. The other children were nominally under the care of Lord Wentworth, but were actually looked after by Thomas Gawdy, an East Anglian adherent of the Howards. In 1548 the custody of all the children was granted to their aunt Mary, duchess of Richmond. In 1550 they moved to Reigate, where Norfolk's half-brother Lord William had created a new mansion from the buildings of a dissolved monastery. In the classroom they were joined by Lord

Wives of the Berkeleys

William's children, including his son Charles, the future Lord Admiral, and his daughter Douglas, named for the king's niece. The manor of Earl Soham, west of Framlingham in Suffolk, was restored to their mother Frances from among the Howard properties to provide her with an income and somewhere to live. Within a short time Frances remarried. Her second husband, the younger son of a Somerset gentleman, was far below her in rank. Little is known of Thomas Steyning before his marriage. It seems likely that he was a sympathetic lawyer, who provided practical help at a particularly difficult time. He proved a more supportive husband than Surrey.

The Duchess of Richmond, who had been personally close to Anne Boleyn, had embraced her cousin's reformist religious views. She employed John Foxe, the humanist scholar and future protestant martyrologist, as tutor to the Howard children. The extent of his influence on the religious views of his young charges is uncertain, but he certainly played an important part in ensuring that they were all well-educated. Like the king's daughters, the girls were taught Latin and became fluent in French and Italian. They were also taught to sing and play the lute. In this way they were prepared to play the roles of leading courtiers for which their birth had destined them. Their aunt occasionally attended court during Edward VI's reign to take part in state occasions, including in 1551 the reception of Mary of Guise, dowager queen of France. However, her precarious finances limited her participation in court life. Within her household the duchess insisted on the strict ceremony appropriate to her status, and the experience of this was important in shaping her charges' own ideas of proper aristocratic behaviour.

Following the accession of Mary I in July 1553 the Duke of Norfolk was released from the Tower and reunited with his grandchildren. He became a member of Mary's council and as earl marshal took a major role in the arrangements for her coronation. At the end of September the queen went to spend the eve of her coronation in the Tower. There, as was customary, she created fifteen new knights of the bath, including Norfolk's seventeen-year-old grandson Thomas and Henry, lord Berkeley, following in his father's and great-uncle's footsteps. Despite Lady Berkeley's earlier association with Anne Boleyn, her conservative views on religion endeared her to the new queen. She was on hand to watch her eighteen-year-old son marking his entry

A Widow and Her Children

into public life by taking an active part in the coronation procession and banquet. Also there to see their brothers playing their parts in the spectacle were Surrey's daughters and Elizabeth Berkeley, who had all recently been introduced to the social life of aristocratic London and the court.[6]

During Mary I's reign Lady Berkeley spent much of her time in London. By the death of Edward VI the lands alienated to the crown three generations before reverted to her son Henry, although as a minor he could not take formal possession of them immediately. In the meantime there were lawyers to consult about the bureaucratic process that would restore Berkeley castle and its estates to the family. At the same time Henry and his sister were launched into society. To provide the family with suitable accommodation in the capital, Anne leased the thirteenth-century house and garden of the bishops of Bangor in Shoe Lane, which ran between Fleet Street and Holborn.

Although some of the Howard lands had been disposed of while the duke was in the Tower, Norfolk managed to recover about two-thirds of his vast estates. He also took over the custody of his grandchildren, replacing the reformist Foxe as their tutor with the conservative John White, who became bishop of Lincoln the following year. Now aged eighty, Norfolk lost no time in negotiating a marriage for his heir. His chosen bride for Thomas was Mary Fitzalan, daughter of Henry, earl of Arundel, who brought extensive estates in Sussex as her inheritance. He also began negotiations with Anne for the marriage of Henry to his grand-daughter, Katherine.

Unlike many young Tudor couples Henry Berkeley and Katherine Howard were able to meet and get to know each other as the marriage negotiations proceeded. They moved within the same tight aristocratic circle in London and encountered each other at court. Katherine was tall with fair hair and a fine complexion. Henry at this time 'frequented the Court, and spent all his time at tenys, bowles, cards, dice, and in the company of his huntsmen and faulkeners'.[7] It was an expensive mode of life, especially for a young man whose estate was reduced by a third to support his mother and his grandfather's widow, Cicely. He also settled £100 a year on his sister Elizabeth, to provide her with an independent income.

In January 1554 a rebellion broke out among those opposed to the queen's proposed marriage to Philip of Spain, led by the courtier and poet Sir Thomas Wyatt. As Norfolk headed to Kent to confront the rebels, Henry received a commission from the queen to raise men in Gloucestershire. He gathered a contingent of five hundred men at Yate and set out for London. The rebellion was over before Henry and his men had got halfway to the capital. It was to be his only military adventure.

At the end of August 1554 the Duke of Norfolk died at Kenninghall. The wording of his will indicates that he was negotiating marriages for all three of Surrey's daughters in the final months of his life. Only that between Katherine and Henry was ready to proceed, as the duke lay dying. The blessing of the union of Henry and Katherine was reportedly one of the old man's final acts. The significance of this touching bedside scene is that it represented a formal betrothal in front of witnesses, which was legally as binding as a church wedding. It meant the marriage settlement was as negotiated by the duke, rather than the £1,000 that Katherine would have inherited under the terms of his will. Smyth's comment that her portion was 'not great', while not putting a figure on it, suggests that it was lower than Katherine's potential inheritance from her grandfather.[8] The couple's quiet wedding took place a few weeks later in the chapel at Kenninghall, while the household remained in deep mourning. Henry then took his place alongside his new brothers-in-law as the funeral procession for the late duke slowly travelled the thirty miles from Kenninghall to Framlingham, where the duke's elaborate funeral took place on 2 October. Afterwards there was a great feast at Framlingham castle. According to the London mercer Henry Machyn, the mourners were fed on 'forty great oxen and a hundred sheep, and sixty calves, besides venison, swans, and cranes, capons, rabbits, pigeons, pikes, and other provisions both flesh and fish'.[9]

Shortly after Norfolk's funeral Henry took Katherine back to London, where they lived in a house on Tower Hill, conveniently placed for taking a boat to any of the royal palaces strung out along the Thames. The queen and her new Spanish husband spent that Christmas at Greenwich, where Henry and Katherine attended the festivities on Twelfth Night. After his marriage the demands on Henry's purse increased, as he and his wife maintained the lifestyle appropriate to their status as leading members of Mary I's court. They employed a hundred and fifty liveried servants, who in summer wore

A Widow and Her Children

tawny-brown cloth coats with a white lion rampant on the left sleeve and in winter white woollen coats lined with crimson taffeta. Attending the court was expensive, but so was travelling to their houses at Mangotsfield, Yate and Caludon, accompanied by their small army of retainers.

Although Berkeley castle was restored to Henry after he came of age at the end of 1555, it did not become his main residence in Gloucestershire. The modern conveniences of Yate were more comfortable than the medieval grandeur of Berkeley. Once Henry gained legal possession of his lands, he increased his mother's jointure. Smyth suggests that Henry was in some way cheated in this transaction, but his mother doubtless felt it only fair that the increase in his estate resulting from the restitution should be reflected by a similar increase in her settlement. She had managed his affairs for two decades and had as his guardian had ample opportunity to enrich herself at his expense. After Henry's marriage Anne retired to Caludon, which had always been her favourite residence. In October 1556 she was granted permission to hear mass in the private chapel there.[10]

By the spring of 1557 Katherine was pregnant with their first child. In June her sister-in-law Mary gave birth to a son, named Philip in honour of the king. The young Duchess of Norfolk died shortly after from puerperal fever. It was a stark reminder for Katherine of the dangers she faced in childbirth. In the first week of October she was taken by litter from Yate to London for the birth. To help allay her natural fears, a respected midwife was fetched from Somerset to attend her. The child was a healthy girl. She was named Mary for the queen, who stood as her godmother. Within a year the Berkeleys' growing debts required some retrenchment. Katherine and Mary went to stay with Katherine's mother at Castle Rising, near King's Lynn in Norfolk. The dowager countess by then had two young children from her second marriage. Acquired by the Howards from the king in 1544, the Norman castle itself at Castle Rising was in a ruinous state. As at Caludon the family's accommodation was in a more comfortable manor house.

While Katherine stayed in Norfolk with their baby, Henry moved from Tower Hill to his mother's house in Shoe Lane. His life of hunting and gambling did not change, but he was able to retrench somewhat by not maintaining his own London house. He first attended parliament in February 1558, although his attendance was intermittent until the queen lay dying in St James's palace that November.

In the period between Mary I's death in mid-November and her funeral a month later, Katherine's brother Norfolk quietly remarried. His bride was Margaret, the nineteen-year-old widow of Henry Dudley, one of the younger sons of the Duke of Northumberland, and the sole heiress of Thomas, lord Audley, a former lord chancellor. Her inheritance included Audley End, where her father had converted the former Walden abbey into a grand house. Lord Audley died in 1544, when Margaret was a child and her wardship was granted to Sir Anthony Denny, a trusted courtier. It was to Denny's house at Cheshunt that Princess Elizabeth was sent in 1548, when Sir Thomas Seymour took too great an interest in her. Margaret had been married to Henry Dudley as soon as she was of age. Shortly after the marriage and before the couple started to co-habit, Edward VI died and Northumberland unsuccessfully attempted to install Margaret's sister-in-law Lady Jane Grey on the throne. With the accession of Mary I Henry and his four brothers were sent to the Tower. Guildford Dudley was executed with his wife following Wyatt's rebellion. John, the eldest of Northumberland's sons, was released when it became obvious he was dying in the autumn of 1554. Henry was probably released at the same time. After England entered the war with France on the side of Spain, Henry was killed at the siege of St Quentin in the summer of 1557. Margaret was just seventeen when Henry Dudley died and had enjoyed little or no married life with her first husband. On the day of her accession Elizabeth I named Robert Dudley as master of the horse. Ambrose Dudley also became a member of the queen's court. In the new reign Norfolk was to have a difficult relationship with his wife's erstwhile brothers-in-law, who he regarded as ambitious upstarts who lacked his family's noble history of service to the crown. There was also a difference in religion, since the Dudleys supported radical protestants, while the Howard circle was religiously conservative. The Berkeleys too would have no love for the Dudleys, their near neighbours in Warwickshire.

~~~

When Elizabeth I ascended to the throne, the status of her Howard kinswomen was enhanced. Katherine was now not only the sister of the leading peer, but second cousin to the queen. Her elder, as yet still unmarried, sister Jane was one of the ladies in attendance on the queen. The Howards, Berkeleys and Dudleys all had a prominent part in the processions, ceremonies and celebrations surrounding Elizabeth's coronation. Also present was the Irish nobleman Thomas Butler, earl of Ormond who would marry Lord Berkeley's sister Elizabeth later that year.

Thomas Butler had been sent to England from Ireland in 1544, to join the circle of young noblemen Henry VIII assembled around his son Edward. He succeeded as Earl of Ormond aged fifteen in 1546, and became a royal ward. As a member of Edward VI's circle he received the finest humanist education available, spending time at Oxford and the inns of court. In the first years of the young king's reign Ormond was a member of the Duke of Somerset's household and was frequently at court. He remained in London after Somerset's fall and in 1551 travelled to France on a diplomatic mission attempting to arrange a marriage between Edward VI and the five-year-old French princess Elizabeth. Although he differed from Mary I in religion, he played a prominent part in defending the queen at the time of the Wyatt rebellion. He spent most of Mary's reign in Ireland, establishing his authority in the area of his family's traditional influence around Kilkenny. He returned to England following Elizabeth I's accession. By then he was approaching thirty and unmarried.

Ormond and Elizabeth Berkeley may first have become acquainted in London, before he returned to Ireland in Mary I's reign. The young earl may also have stayed with Lady Berkeley at either Bristol or Caludon, when travelling between London and Ireland. Elizabeth was reputedly very attractive, but her comparative lack of dowry was a discouragement to potential suitors and at twenty-five she remained unmarried. His upbringing led Ormond to prefer an English bride, but few fathers were overly keen to see their daughters marry an Irish lord. As Elizabeth was prepared to live in Ireland and Ormond did not need a rich bride, the marriage suited them both and was quickly arranged. Ormond was prominent at court during the early months of the reign, and in July 1559 he was one of the three challengers at a joust at Greenwich. The following month he was appointed lord treasurer of Ireland. When he left England to take up his new position, Elizabeth accompanied him as Countess of Ormond. The speed of their departure meant that the details of Elizabeth's jointure, which was to be drawn from land in Ireland, were not agreed until some time later.

By the middle of 1559 Lord Berkeley was feeling financially more secure, as the death of his grandfather's widow Cicely further increased his income.[11] He removed his family from Castle Rising to Caludon and ordered his hounds to be sent from Yate. He and Katherine spent the summer buck hunting in the great deer parks of Warwickshire and Leicestershire. Both Henry and Katherine adored hunting. She was adept with both the crossbow and the longbow. They also kept merlins for hunting, which were sometimes housed in Katherine's chamber to the despair of those responsible for her clothes and the room's furnishings. For over a decade each summer was spent in a similar way, either in Warwickshire, Gloucestershire or with her brother in his various houses with their extensive deer parks. During the winter months Henry and Katherine were frequently at court, although Christmas would be spent at their main residence with their children. Their income still proving insufficient, this way of life was maintained by the regular sale of land and manors from Henry's inheritance.

Henry and Katherine celebrated Christmas at Yate in 1559 in great style, entertaining the local gentry with a lavish hospitality that was allegedly remembered for over half a century. Until 1564 Yate Court was the couple's main residence and their next three children were born there. A male heir Ferdinand was born early in 1560. This coincided with the negotiations between Elizabeth I and the Habsburg emperor Ferdinand over her proposed marriage to his younger son, the Archduke Charles. Norfolk was an outspoken supporter of this match, which would stymie Robert Dudley's ambition to marry the queen. Henry and Katherine's unusual choice of name suggests that the Imperial ambassador stood as godfather, possibly as a proxy for the emperor. Frances, named for the dowager Countess of Surrey, was born in 1561 and the queen stood as her godmother. Another daughter, Katherine, followed in 1562. Norfolk's family was also expanding during these years, as Margaret produced four children before her death in 1563. Early death was a constant factor in sixteenth-century lives from which no-one was immune and infant mortality was particularly rife. The Berkeley heir Ferdinand died at the age of two and was buried at Yate. His sister Katherine also died in early infancy, as did one of Norfolk's daughters. When Henry's mother died in 1564, he sold the remainder of the lease of Yate to his cousin Sir Nicholas Poyntz. Thereafter Caludon was the couple's main residence and it was there in 1566 that Katherine gave birth to their daughter Jane.

During these years both Katherine's sisters were married to northern lords. The younger, Margaret married Henry, lord Scrope. A widower in his early twenties with a young daughter, he attended Elizabeth I's coronation and that summer took part in the formal ceremony at St Paul's marking the death of the French king Henri II. The following winter he was involved in besieging Leith as part of a campaign led by Norfolk against the Auld Alliance of France and Scotland. In January 1561 he was appointed to the Council of the North and his marriage to Margaret appears to have taken place around this time. In April 1563 he became captain of Carlisle castle and warden of the West Marches. His mother Lady Scrope was a staunch catholic who sheltered priests in her house at Whitby, but Scrope's loyalty to the queen was unquestioned. Katherine's elder sister Jane married Charles Neville, who became earl of Westmorland in 1564. They were second cousins, both their paternal grandmothers being daughters of the Duke of Buckingham. Indeed the marital problems of the Norfolk's grandfather were said to stem initially from Elizabeth Stafford having been expecting and keen to marry Westmorland's grandfather, when the duke intervened and the earl married her younger sister instead.

After their marriages both her sisters and her sister-in-law took precedence over Katherine. Jane was married to an English earl, while Elizabeth's earl, although Irish and hence of lower significance, was related to the queen through her mother. Margaret's husband was a baron of higher precedence than Lord Berkeley, who also held important positions for the defence of the realm. In the world of formal ceremony in which the women moved, this mattered. Strict hierarchical order was observed not simply on state occasions, when the aristocracy presented a public image of stability. It was observed within noble households as well. When staying with the duke at

Kenninghall, Katherine would enter the great hall for formal meals after either of her sisters, be sat further away from their brother and be served later.

Once in Ireland the romance of Elizabeth Berkeley's whirlwind courtship and marriage to the dark-haired, dashing Ormond was replaced by the reality of living in a strange country, where she did not speak the language. While her husband was busy with his official duties and often absent, Elizabeth became lonely and bored. Nor did she have the consolation of a nursery filling with children to distract her. While her sister-in-law Katherine produced a baby regularly each year, after four years of marriage Elizabeth had not given her husband an heir, nor seemed likely to do so. By the spring of 1564 the marriage had broken down. Reports reached Henry that his sister was being badly treated by her husband. When the lord deputy, Katherine's cousin Thomas, earl of Sussex, was summoned to London that May, Henry sought his help as a mediator between the couple. The result was a formal separation, referred to as a divorce from bed and board. Elizabeth returned to England. To counter accusations that he had mistreated Elizabeth, her husband revealed some letters she had exchanged with other men. The 'great folly' Elizabeth had demonstrated lost her support, although she may have been guilty of no more than the flirtatious behaviour that was common at the English court. Her indiscretion might have been overlooked and the marriage survived, if she had not been childless. It was as the failure of her daughter's marriage became public knowledge, that Anne died at Caludon and was buried in St Michael's, Coventry.[12]

Ormond was keen to procure a full divorce, that would allow him to remarry. In an earlier age Elizabeth might have been persuaded to enter a convent, but this was no longer available as a means of terminating an inconvenient marriage. Ormond had no great difficulty in obtaining judgement in his favour in Ireland. However, with the support of her extended family Elizabeth successfully appealed to the English privy council to deny Ormond a divorce. In 1566, when Robert Dudley, by then Earl of Leicester, was briefly out of favour, Ormond became the new royal favourite and the queen's chief male companion at state ceremonials. His intimate relationship with the queen did not, however, procure him a divorce. Elizabeth I notoriously preferred her favourites to remain unmarried or to have wives who did not appear at court. Eventually a settlement was reached in 1569, which confirmed the couple's separation but prevented Thomas from remarrying while Elizabeth lived. She received a pension from her estranged husband of £90 a year for life, which was equivalent to the income many aristocratic widows could expect from their jointures. However, unlike a widow she was reliant on a resentful husband, whose payment of her annuity was often tardy. On occasion Elizabeth had to ask her brother to remind her husband of his obligations. She retired to the house leased by her mother in Bristol. There her uncertain status as a discarded countess was bolstered by the strong ties of her paternal family to the city and the neighbouring gentry. Life as the head of her own household was no doubt preferable to continuing within a marriage that had irretrievably broken down and Elizabeth was fortunate to have the status, family and friends to arrange this.

3 Mary, Queen of Scots and the Howards

As warden of the West Marches Margaret Howard's husband Lord Scrope was inevitably drawn into the turbulent politics of Scotland. In October 1565 he provided sanctuary to James Stewart, earl of Moray, following his defeat by his half-sister Mary, Queen of Scots in the Chaseabout Raid. Two years later Mary was forced to abdicate in favour of her son and imprisoned in Loch Leven castle. In May 1568 she escaped. Defeated in battle by Moray, she fled to England, hoping that her cousin Elizabeth I would help restore her to the Scottish throne. Having crossed the Solway Firth, Mary spent the night at Workington Hall before being conducted to Carlisle castle by Scrope's deputy. She was never to return to Scotland. When news of Mary's arrival in Carlisle reached London, the privy council ordered Scrope and Sir Francis Knollys to take charge of Mary, being anxious to prevent her finding refuge with the catholic Earl of Northumberland. Once they had Mary in protective custody, the privy council was uncertain what to do about the queen's unwelcome guest. Elizabeth I understandably strongly disapproved of the overthrow of an anointed queen. However, she and her council preferred Scotland to be under the control of protestant lords looking for support rather than the pro-French, catholic Mary. Access to the Scottish queen was initially quite relaxed. On 15 June Scrope accompanied her outside the castle to attend a football match, and the local nobility and gentry were allowed to visit her. By the middle of July with local catholics flocking to pay homage to the exiled queen, the privy council became concerned about their ability to keep control of the situation. They ordered Scrope to move Mary away from the border region to his castle further south at Bolton in Wensleydale.

The previous year the Duke of Norfolk had strengthened the Howard ties with the northern nobility by marrying Elizabeth, the daughter of Sir James Leyburne of Kendal and widow of Thomas, lord Dacre of Gilsland. The marriage took place quietly at the home of Elizabeth's widowed mother Lady Leyburne. By her first husband Elizabeth was the mother of the heir to the Dacre lordship and three daughters, who would each have a substantial dowry. She came from a staunchly catholic family. The Howard circle as a whole, including the Berkeleys, tended towards conservative religious views; however, they generally attended church services, at least when at court, and avoided overt recusancy. Despite his own conformity Norfolk seems to have been unworried about the potential influence of an overtly catholic wife on their children. With some difficulty the duke obtained the wardship of the Dacre children and planned to absorb their inheritance into the Howard estate by a sequence of marriages between them and his own children. Elizabeth died in childbirth just seven months after their marriage. The catholic influence on her children and stepchildren was, however, continued by the active involvement of Lady Leyburne in their upbringing. Her son died from a fall in 1569, bringing the Dacre lordship to an end and leaving his three sisters as his extremely lucrative co-heirs.

Of a similar age to the Scottish queen and a young mother herself, Lady Scrope was sympathetic to her husband's unwanted guest. Once the Queen of Scots was settled at Bolton, it became apparent that Norfolk would be appointed to the commission investigating the charges against her. Margaret conveyed messages of encouragement to Mary from her brother and was probably the first to suggest that Mary and Norfolk might marry. That October Norfolk and the other commissioners met representatives of the new Scottish government at York. One day, when he was out hawking with one of the Scottish representatives, it was suggested to Norfolk that he should marry Mary. This was presented as a way of restoring Mary to her throne under the influence of a protestant husband, of furthering the alliance between England and Scotland, and of consolidating Mary's claim as heir to the English throne. Although Mary was still married to the Earl of Bothwell, this was not seen as a significant impediment. Mary and her catholic supporters had little regard for a marriage conducted under protestant rites and were prepared to argue that the queen had been coerced by Bothwell. Norfolk's marriage to Elizabeth Dacre had shown that he in his turn was not troubled by the prospect of a catholic wife. Potentially more problematic was his belief that the notorious 'casket letters', some of which he'd been shown a few days before, were genuine and demonstrated Mary's complicity in the death of Bothwell's predecessor Lord Darnley.

Norfolk had been one of the English peers suggested as a possible husband for Mary, before the queen had made her own impetuous choice of Darnley. That was at a time when the Scottish queen sat securely on her own throne and Elizabeth I was keen to foster good relations. Now the situation was very different. Norfolk might picture himself helping Mary to regain her throne and himself wearing the crown matrimonial. Elizabeth was at best ambivalent about restoring her Francophile cousin. Moreover with the captive queen providing a focus for catholic dissent, it was inevitable that Elizabeth and her council would oppose Mary's marriage to Norfolk, with his wealth, flexibility with regard to religion, and a clientele that alone would constitute a small army.

Neither belief in Mary's guilt nor Elizabeth I's almost certain displeasure apparently discouraged Norfolk from pursuing the idea of marriage with a woman he had never met. At the same time he was not prepared to acknowledge it openly, although the idea was common currency within his immediate circle. When rumours concerning the proposed marriage spread more widely, Elizabeth challenged Norfolk directly about them. He denied there was any truth in the rumours and was left in no doubt of the queen's violent disapproval. Soon after this Mary was moved from Bolton further south to Tutbury and the communication link through Lady Scrope was lost.

While Norfolk continued to contemplate the restoration of Mary to the Scottish throne with himself as her consort, by the spring of 1569 a group of leading catholics led by the Earl of Arundel had more radical plans. They were conspiring to liberate Mary, place her on the English throne with Norfolk as her husband, and restore the country's allegiance to the papacy. The Earl of Westmorland was one of the leading conspirators, although Jane and her husband did not at first tell Norfolk about the planned rebellion and his role in it. Norfolk was finally brought into the conspiracy during his annual hunting progress, on which he was accompanied by the Berkeleys and the Scropes. Secrecy and discretion were not the hallmarks of these conspirators. As the hunting parties continued, all the participants would have become aware something was afoot. Lord Scrope was honour bound to report any rumours or suspicions to the privy council. Failing to do so would have risked not only his career, but the future of his family. All Norfolk's immediate circle were endangered by the Westmorlands' plotting, as they hunted and feasted their way around the deer parks of north-east England that summer.

Mary, Queen of Scots and the Howards

Through the reports of officers in the North like Scrope, the queen and her ministers were fully aware of the threat of an uprising in Mary's favour and the intended role of the duke. That summer Norfolk was given several opportunities by Elizabeth I to confess his plans to marry the Scottish queen. A confession might have nipped the whole affair in the bud, but Norfolk failed to take advantage of those opportunities. Lacking the nerve to either confess all to the queen or to proceed with the conspiracy, Norfolk retreated to Kenninghall. Around this time he married his eldest son Philip to his step-daughter Anne Dacre. Although Philip was below the legal age of consent, this was the best Norfolk could do to protect him from the perils of wardship. Norfolk was clearly preparing against the possibility of his own destruction. When the duke retired to Norfolk, Elizabeth I feared and Mary's supporters hoped he was about to raise an army in the Howard heartlands. At the final moment Norfolk baulked at outright rebellion. Summoned by the queen to join the court at Windsor, he attempted to delay but did not refuse to go. Instead he sent a message to the conspirators to call off their rising. When he pleaded with Westmorland specifically to stay at home, his sister Jane unsympathetically commented: 'what a simple man the Duke is to begin a matter and not go through with it'. His elder sister was made of sterner stuff.[1]

As Norfolk made his way slowly towards Windsor at the beginning of October, orders came that he should be taken instead to Burnham Abbey, which lay a few miles upstream. He was held there for eight days, before Elizabeth I finally agreed that he should be sent to the Tower. The protection a number of catholics had received in Norfolk's household was shattered, as they were required to attend church and to take communion. His sons' tutor fled the country and was subsequently ordained as a priest. The Berkeleys, implicated by accompanying Norfolk north to hunt that summer, were consigned to the custody of the sheriff of Worcestershire, Sir Thomas Russell. Their sojourn at Strensham was later presented by Smyth as an economic measure, but it was enforced not voluntary. They were under a form of house arrest. At the same time Katherine's brother Henry Howard was in the custody of the Archbishop of Canterbury at Lambeth. During the previous summer he had produced a treatise on natural and moral philosophy for Katherine, in apparent anticipation that his

45

sister might need something to occupy her time.

While rumours of a catholic rising continued to circulate in the North, the Earl of Sussex as president of the council at York took a relaxed approach. In September he invited the earls of Northumberland and Westmorland and all the principal gentlemen of the area and their wives to a week's hunting party at Cawood castle. Jane Neville was absent from her cosin's social event, being either about to give birth or recently delivered of a son. In October Sussex was ordered by the queen, who took a less sanguine view of the rumours, to send for the earls and in her name summon them to court. Northumberland temporised, but Westmorland, his resolve stiffened by his indomitable wife, sent a blank refusal: 'I dare not come where my enemies are without bringing such a force to protect me as might be misliked; therefore I think it better to stay at home'. In November Northumberland joined Westmorland and a band of supporters at Brancepeth for a council of war. When the men seemed to be wavering in their determination to rebel, Jane in tears harangued them : 'We and our country were shamed for ever, that now in the end we should seek holes to creep into'. The countess of Northumberland was also reputed to have been more determined than her husband. Despite being pregnant, the next day she accompanied the men as they rode to Durham. Having stormed the cathedral, the rebels proceeded south. They got within striking distance of Tutbury, but the Scottish queen had been moved out of harm's way to Coventry. Denied their principal target and with the foreign aid they had expected failing to materialise, the rebellion fizzled out. Westmorland and the Northumberlands fled to Scotland. All three were named in the subsequent act of attainder.[2]

Following the flight of the earls, Jane was left in a state of suspense at Brancepeth. Sir John Constable, who had married Westmorland's sister, was sent to persuade Jane to write a letter to her husband asking him to return. This she did and handed the letter over to Sir John unsealed, so he could confirm its contents. In February 1570 Robert Constable, an English spy who had seen her husband in Scotland, arrived at the castle bringing a ring as a token from Westmorland. When Jane, who was naturally wary of unexpected visitors, finally agreed to speak to him Constable described her as 'passing joyful' to receive word from her husband. He was clearly impressed by Jane's intelligence and spirit, reporting that 'for ripeness of wit, readiness of memory, and plain and pithy utterance of her words, I have talked with many, but never her like'.[3] Jane gave Constable a diamond ring and several other pieces of jewellery, that Westmorland would be able to sell to pay his expenses in Scotland. Constable also hoped to acquire ciphers used by the conspirators in their communications. Wary of handing over evidence that could incriminate others to a stranger, Jane claimed the ciphers had been buried by a servant. As the servant was conveniently absent, the ciphers could not be retrieved. The following month Jane travelled to London. From the Charterhouse, Norfolk's London home, she wrote to William Cecil. She sought the queen's leading councillor's help in obtaining an audience with the queen, so she could plead the case for her and her children in person.

In August 1570 Norfolk was released from the Tower to house arrest. Jane remained with him at the Charterhouse, continuing her quest to rescue the fortunes of her children from the wreck of the rebellion. As a result of Westmorland's attainder, all his property was forfeited and his children disinherited, as she and her siblings had been in their own childhood. Her son died before he was two, leaving Jane with four daughters. Her husband meanwhile escaped from Scotland and took refuge in the Spanish Netherlands. They were never to meet again.

Whether through arrogance or stupidity Norfolk's imprisonment failed to teach him caution and he continued to entertain hopes of marrying the Scottish queen. While under house arrest, he became embroiled in the intrigues around Mary known as the Ridolfi Plot. The Ridolfi conspirators planned to assassinate Elizabeth I and place Mary on the throne in her place. Jane had good reason to encourage the conspiracy. As the wife of a convicted traitor she was in an awkward position. The only way her position within society would be re-established and the future of her daughters secured was for Mary to replace Elizabeth I on the throne. Then her husband would be able to return to England, receive a pardon and recover his estates. The presence of Jane at the Charterhouse helps to explain how Norfolk allowed himself to become entangled with Ridolfi. The Berkeleys were also in London during the late spring of 1571, as a bill concerning Katherine's jointure was before parliament. Henry, despairing of having a son, had decided to settle his estate on his three surviving daughters.

The queen's progress that summer included Audley End in Essex, which the second of Norfolk's three sons, Thomas, had inherited through his mother. While she was there, 'great means were used' to persuade Elizabeth I to release Norfolk from house arrest and his supporters believed the queen was sympathetic. Unfortunately news arrived from London of the overwhelming evidence for the duke's involvement in the Ridolfi Plot.[4] Norfolk was arrested and returned to the Tower in September. Four months later he was convicted of treason and sentenced to death. The Berkeleys apparently again spent time in the custody of Sir Thomas Russell.

Elizabeth I was extremely reluctant to sign her cousin's death warrant, but was eventually persuaded. Norfolk was executed in June 1572. After his execution Lady Berkeley 'retired herself into her chamber and private walks', mourning her brother and the effect of his conviction on their wider family.[5] Her sister Jane went to live in one of the Howard manorhouses in Norfolk, where her uncertain status as the wife of a traitor was bolstered by her paternal family's strong, local links. Eventually Elizabeth I granted annuities of £300 for the maintenance of Westmorland's daughters.

~~~

Norfolk's fall inevitably cast a shadow over his family and close associates. His fifteen-year-old son and heir Philip did not inherit the title, although he was allowed to retain a large proportion of the family property. Much of the responsibility for the management of his affairs was taken by Roger Townshend of Raynham, a leading Norfolk gentleman whose family had a long association with the Howards. Philip's younger brothers were committed to Townshend's care under the guardianship of the queen's chief minister William Cecil. In time they married their Dacre step-sisters, as Norfolk intended. Thanks to his strategic marriages, Norfolk's children had inheritances through their mothers that were untouched by his attainder. This included Audley End, where a household was established for them. Norfolk's younger brother Henry became dependent on the generosity of his family, including a small pension from Lady Berkeley.

For the Berkeleys Norfolk's fall led to the revival of a troublesome lawsuit. Although the family had eventually emerged victorious from the fifteenth-century dispute over the possession of their lands, the rival claim was not forgotten. By the Tudor period it had descended to the Duke of Northumberland and, following his execution for treason, to the crown. This claim would have foundered, if on reaching his majority Henry had received his lands as a new grant from Mary I. However, insisting on a restitution rather than a new grant allowed the Berkeleys to recover leases agreed while the land was out of their hands. This was an important financial consideration in light of Henry and Katherine's lavish lifestyle. It was probably the need to raise money rather than Anne's 'womanishe willfullnesse', as Smyth claimed, that led Henry's mother to insist on the lands being restored as of right rather than newly granted.[6] As a result, the rival claim remained. Although the queen's lawyers initiated proceedings in the Exchequer court to establish the crown's continuing claim, no further action was taken until Norfolk's execution. Then the Earl of Leicester, Northumberland's son, instigated the prosecution of the royal claim. If he succeeded, the queen promised to restore the lands to his family.

Under the circumstances Lady Berkeley would have been well-advised to behave circumspectly, but she was not immune from the Howard curse of haughty arrogance and overweening pride. She was far better educated than her husband and considered herself better equipped to deal with legal and financial matters. She was not a wife who thought that her husband knew best or would accept his decisions unquestioningly. During the period when Norfolk was in trouble, but not yet convicted of treason, Leicester and his brother Ambrose, earl of Warwick had suggested that her two eldest daughters Mary and Frances should marry their nephews Sir Philip and Sir Robert Sidney. The settlement of the Berkeley estate on his daughters in 1571 was devised to prevent their descent to the male heir, Henry's cousin Edward Berkeley, who would inherit the title. Ironically this mirrored the situation that had caused the original problem in the fifteenth century, the Dudleys' ancestress having opposed the transfer of her father's estate to Henry's ancestor, the heir male. The proposed marriages would have provided a means to consolidate the existing rival claims, although at the risk of raising a new claimant in the shape of Edward Berkeley. The couples were compatible in age and, although the boys' father Sir Henry Sidney was a hard-working civil servant rather than a peer, their prospects as the

Dudley heirs enhanced their status. Yet, despite the dangers inherent in her brother's position at that time, Katherine refused to countenance the proposal as being beneath her daughters.

In a doomed attempt to combat her opposition Lord Berkeley sought the support of his kinsmen among the greater gentry of Gloucestershire. Their written recommendation in the autumn of 1573 made it clear that their preference would be for the Berkeley lands to descend with the title to the male heir. Edward Berkeley was a known quantity and a Gloucestershire man. The Sidney brothers had no direct interests in the county and, like Henry since he moved to Caludon, were unlikely to spend much time there or play an active part in county affairs. If Henry insisted on leaving his estate to his daughters, then his kinsmen thought the Sidney marriages should be pursued, provided the terms were acceptable. Lady Berkeley, Surrey's daughter and as stubborn as her sister Jane, was not to be swayed by the opinion of the local gentry and remained vehemently opposed. Her opposition was no doubt further strengthened by Leicester's cavalier behaviour towards her cousin and former schoolfellow Douglas, now the widowed Lady Sheffield, who in the winter of 1573 was carrying his child.

Pressure in favour of the Sidney marriages continued to be applied. The following spring the queen made it plain, that her favour was not going to be easily recovered. In the course of seeking a pardon for arrears claimed by the Exchequer, Katherine petitioned the queen on her knees. Elizabeth I was reported to have responded to her plea with the words 'Noe noe, my lady Berkeley, wee know you will never love us for the death of your brother'.[7] At around the same time the Berkeleys' youngest daughter Jane died, aged eight. Apparently she ate a baked apple prepared by the gardener with arsenic to poison rats, although the servants kept this from her grieving parents. That summer the Berkeleys remained at Caludon, as the queen visited Gloucestershire during her summer progress. In August she stayed with Henry's cousin Sir Nicholas Poyntz at Iron Acton. Leicester, intending to increase the pressure on the Berkeleys, arranged a hunt for the queen in the park at Berkeley. When news reached Henry that twenty-seven of his stags had been killed, he was furious. Declaring that the hunting at Berkeley had been ruined by such carnage, he threatened to destroy the park altogether. As Henry was subsequently warned by a friend at court, this was exactly the response the earl had hoped to provoke. It meant he could whisper in the queen's ear that Berkeley's reaction to her day's sport was disloyal and possibly even treasonous.

At the beginning of 1575 the faltering negotiations with the Dudleys were put on ice, when Lady Berkeley announced that she was pregnant again. The marriage proposal depended upon the girls being their father's co-heirs, so once there was the prospect of a son and heir, negotiations were suspended. In her desperation to produce a son, Katherine had taken advice from one of her retainers. Francis Aylworth was a little, sickly old man, but well-educated and experienced as a surgeon and physician. Katherine persuaded her husband that they should follow Aylworth's advice to enhance their chances of producing a son and heir. The nature of the advice they received is a mystery, but Katherine had good reason to believe that it was effective. In July 1575 after twenty-one years of marriage and nine years after her last child was born, Katherine produced a son. The birth of Thomas scuppered any prospect of an immediate end to the dispute with the Dudleys. The queen, who was visiting Leicester at Kenilworth when Thomas was born six miles away at Caludon, agreed to stand as godmother. Ironically Anne, countess of Warwick was sent to act as the queen's deputy at the christening. As a result of Thomas's birth the countess would be embroiled in the ongoing lawsuit for the rest of her life.

~~~

In 1578 Norfolk's sons acted as hosts to the queen at Audley End, Kenninghall and Mount Surrey outside Norwich during her summer progress to East Anglia. Philip Howard had lived predominantly in London since leaving Cambridge in 1576 and the royal visit may have been the first time he had returned to Kenninghall since his father's arrest. During that summer negotiations were proceeding for a possible marriage between Elizabeth I and Francois, duc d'Alençon, the younger brother of the French king. The Howards supported the French match, with Lady Berkeley's brother Henry writing a tract in its favour. In part their support was rooted in the blow such a marriage would give to Leicester's position.

Following the death of his first wife Amy Robsart, Leicester had entertained hopes of persuading Elizabeth I to marry him. While

Wives of the Berkeleys

hostile rumours surrounding the circumstances of Amy's death and the opposition of leading members of the privy council combined with the queen's own doubts to prevent her marrying her favourite, Leicester knew she would take violent exception to his marrying anyone else. His affair with the widowed Lady Sheffield had produced an illegitimate son, but neither Leicester nor his brother Warwick had a legitimate son to perpetuate the Dudley line. In 1575 there were rumours in London of an affair between Leicester and Lettice, countess of Essex, while her husband was in Ireland. Lettice was a close relative of the queen, being the granddaughter of Mary Boleyn. Moreover, it was strongly suspected that her mother Katherine, who had been close to Elizabeth I as a lady of the bedchamber until her death in 1569, was the illegitimate daughter of Henry VIII. Essex died the following year, making only a perfunctory reference to his wife in his will. In September 1578, once Lettice's jointure was settled and she had observed a respectable two years of mourning, she quietly married Leicester. Although the wedding had been discreet, it quickly became widely known. When the queen found out is uncertain. According to the Spanish ambassador, the beans were spilt in December 1579 by Jean de Simier, who was wooing the queen on behalf of Alençon. Whether that was when Elizabeth I found out, when she chose to reveal her knowledge, or when she learnt about Lady Sheffield and her son is not clear. What is certain is that thereafter the queen's relationship with Leicester was never quite the same and his countess was unwelcome at court.

Around this time Lady Berkeley decided to ask a local wise man to cast a horoscope. In the sixteenth century a belief in astrology was not unusual. It was widely regarded as an effective way of predicting the future and was common at all levels of society from the queen down. Puritans disapproved, regarding astrology as a popish practice, but they were a small minority – although comparatively strong in Coventry. So Lady Berkeley's request was not in itself strange or unusual. Katherine entrusted her bailiff John Bott with a letter to a wise man called Bourne, who lived in the Forest of Arden. The bailiff was a convenient courier, as he travelled around the Midlands collecting rents and organising supplies for the household. His relationship with Katherine would not have been close, and she would not have expected him to read her letter or the written response. The letter presumably asked Bourne whether Leicester would be restored to favour with the queen, a question of immense and immediate interest to the Berkeleys and the Howards. Rumours reported by the Spanish ambassador concerning Leicester's alleged hopes of marrying Lettice's children to potential claimants to the throne may well have reached him through Katherine's brother Henry. Such rumours were clearly designed to damage Leicester. Given the influence Leicester wielded even when under a cloud, Katherine understandably wanted no documentary evidence of her enquiry. So she told Bott to make sure that he saw Bourne burn her letter. Years later she would have reason to wish she had chosen a more reliable courier.

In 1578 the Howards had expended vast sums of money, entertaining the queen on her East Anglian progress. When the queen's French suitor, by then Duc d'Anjou, returned to England in 1581, the Howard family and their relations played prominent roles. This too came at an exorbitant cost. As the prince was travelling with only a small entourage, Elizabeth I ordered various members of the English aristocracy to attend on him during his stay. These included Philip, who had succeeded his maternal grandfather as earl of Arundel the year before, his brothers William and Thomas, and his uncle Henry. Lord Berkeley and his wife were also ordered to attend the prince, presumably because Katherine like her brother and nephews was fluent in French. While in London the Berkeleys stayed at Ivy Bridge, off the Strand and close to Whitehall, where Katherine's nephew William Howard had a house inherited by his step-sister and wife Elizabeth Dacre. Attendance on the French prince was extremely expensive, costing the Berkeleys £2,500 according to Smyth, and stretched their already over-burdened finances.

While the queen famously did not wish to open windows into men's souls, she did require outward conformity in matters of religion. Peers in particular were expected to set an example to their retainers and wider society. Katherine's brother Henry, although his catholic beliefs were an open secret, attended the royal chapel when at court to demonstrate his loyalty. By 1581 both the earl of Arundel and his wife Anne had become catholics, although Philip was not formally accepted into the church and attempted for three years to follow the same politic line as his uncle. Anne meanwhile made no secret of her

Wives of the Berkeleys

beliefs and would not attend an Anglican service. In 1583 the queen lost her patience with the countess, who was committed to house arrest for a year with Sir Thomas Shirley at Wiston, Sussex. While in custody she gave birth to a daughter.

During this time the Berkeleys went to stay for an extended period at Beaurepaire, Hampshire, a newly-built mansion belonging to Henry's first cousin, Sir John Savage. Although Sir John had inherited a much reduced estate in Cheshire, the influence of his mother's family, his marriage to a daughter of the Earl of Rutland, and years of diligent public service had repaired much of the damage done by his grandfather and father. He had acquired Beaurepaire and the hereditary office of master of the royal buckhounds through his second wife Eleanor, the widow and executrix of Sir Richard Pecksall. During their stay with Savage the Berkeley household was reduced by twenty servants, although it quickly returned to its former strength when they moved on. Smyth represented their sojourn in Hampshire as a period of economic retrenchment, which was certainly welcome after their recent expenses and the need to find money for their daughters' dowries. However, there may also have been an element of the Berkeleys being kept under observation by Elizabeth I's council due to concerns about the loyalty of the Howards and their circle.

On Valentine's day 1584, following the family's departure from Hampshire, the Berkeleys' elder daughter Mary married John, the son of Sir John Zouch of Codnor, Derbyshire at Caludon. She was almost thirty, while John was just twenty. John's father had been made a knight of the bath at Elizabeth I's coronation and, as a reliable protestant, been called upon to assist those in charge of guarding the Queen of Scots. Although he had inherited a large estate, Sir John had run up considerable debts through his involvement in lead mining. Mary Berkeley brought her husband a much-needed dowry of £2,500 and a further £500 worth of jewels and fine clothes. In return land worth an estimated £500 a year was placed in trust for her jointure. The match may have been promoted by the Howard's agent Roger Townshend, whose wife's family lived close to Codnor. The following year Lord Berkeley would sell the castle and manor of Bretby in Derbyshire to Sir Thomas Stanhope of Shelford, Nottinghamshire, Townshend's brother-in-law.

Once Mary was married, the Berkeleys moved from Caludon to live at the Whitefriars, Coventry, while extensive building works were going on at the castle. The work involved the re-roofing and internal restructuring of the medieval castle to allow the family more privacy. The porter's lodge, brewhouse, stables and other outbuildings were completely rebuilt. The Whitefriars, which they leased for three years, was a grand house incorporating part of the former monastic cloisters. The queen herself had stayed there in 1565. Until this time their son Thomas had lived within his mother's household, being thoroughly spoilt and taught comparatively little. It was usual for sons to leave their mother's sphere at the age of seven, but the length of time she had waited for her son and the early death of three of his siblings made Katherine reluctant to surrender her care of him. It was only when he was nine and the family had moved to Coventry, that a tutor from Oxford was engaged and a distant relative brought into the household to share his lessons. It was at this time that John Smyth joined the household from the grammar school at Derby as a servant to Thomas. Smyth also joined the lessons, this being a cost-effective way of training up a retainer to serve the family. The schoolroom was closely overseen and controlled by Lady Berkeley. While living at Whitefriars, Thomas fell and suffered an injury that left his neck and head permanently awry. Thereafter Katherine was even more solicitous for her late, miracle child.

After his wife was released from house arrest, the Earl of Arundel was formally accepted into the catholic church in September 1584. The following April, faced with the choice of maintaining the level of outward conformity acceptable to the queen or perpetual house arrest, he took the desperate decision to flee abroad. Anne was then pregnant, their son being born in July. Arrested on board ship, Philip was taken to the Tower and tried in Star Chamber on charges of being a catholic, fleeing England without the queen's permission, intriguing with Jesuit priests and claiming title to the dukedom of Norfolk. In 1586 he was fined heavily and detained at the queen's pleasure. The countess remained at liberty, although the government remained suspicious of her loyalty. Their doubts were magnified when they intercepted a letter from an agent of Mary, Queen of Scots, which suggested the exiled queen might use the countess and her Dacre connections as a conduit for letters into Scotland. Despite the potential dangers Anne supported the Jesuit priest Robert Southwell and allowed him to set up a secret press in a house she owned in London. It is perhaps surprising that the privy council allowed this uncompromising catholic to retain custody of her two children.

In February 1586 the Berkeley's younger daughter Frances married George Shirley of Staunton Harold, Leicestershire at Caludon. George had inherited a large estate from his grandfather as a boy in 1571. His wardship was acquired by Sir John Throckmorton, a younger brother of Henry's uncle by marriage. Sir John doubtless intended to marry this wealthy young man to one of his daughters. However, when he was in urgent need of money, he accepted £1,500 from George in exchange for allowing him to choose his own bride. In 1584 Sir John's son Francis Throckmorton became involved in a plot to free Mary, Queen of Scots and was executed. During the investigation of the plot George was questioned about his close association with Francis and his own religious conformity. This experience encouraged him to demonstrate his loyalty by serving in the Netherlands with Leicester's army in 1585. Like her sister, Frances had a dowry of £2,500. When the couple married, Henry sold the Leicestershire manor of Sileby to his new son-in-law for £3,200. While her sister Mary's marriage took her to a strange county, where her staunchly protestant husband would inherit an indebted estate, Frances married a wealthy man, who shared her religious inclinations and kinship circle. Smyth recorded that he had 'seldom known a more true wedlocke nor more tender love in marriage'.[8] The couple had five children during their nine years of marriage. Frances was a steadfast catholic and brought up her children in the same religion. Her husband meanwhile practised the minimal conformity that was required to avoid trouble. Frances died from puerperal fever in 1595, leaving two sons and a daughter. Three years after her death George married Dorothy, the widow of the Elizabethan diplomat Sir Henry Unton.

~~~

In the febrile atmosphere surrounding Arundel's imprisonment, the trial and execution of the Queen of Scots, and the subsequent preparations for defending England against the Spanish Armada, a rumour began to circulate about the earlier casting of a horoscope for Lady Berkeley. What in other circumstances would have been an unremarkable use of astrology for an Elizabethan noblewoman became the cause of suspicion and danger. Unfortunately for

Katherine, her letter to the astrologer Bourne had not been burnt, but rather kept by her bailiff. Bott was later sacked and required to account for the money he had collected and disbursed as bailiff. Unable to produce an adequate set of accounts, he used the letter to blackmail Katherine. He went to Whitefriars to confront her, accompanied by William Phines, a Coventry merchant. Although Bott did not manage to keep his position as bailiff, his neighbours noticed that proceedings against him were dropped and he was not pursued for his rent arrears. Phines was initially happy to benefit from having Katherine's favour in return for his discretion. However, as Bott began to mutter darkly that he knew things that could cost Katherine her head, Phines began to fear coming under suspicion of being an accessory to treason. In 1581 it had become a statutory felony to erect figures, cast nativities, or calculate by prophecy how long the queen would live or who would succeed her. According to his later evidence, Phines came to believe the letter had not been about Leicester but rather about the queen.[9]

The rumours surrounding Bott eventually reached his landlord, Phines's nephew Christopher Wade. Wade was the son of a Coventry mercer and a fellow of Magdalen College, Oxford. His family had prospered in the sixteenth century, when his grandfather served as mayor of Coventry and his father acquired former monastic lands. However, various lawsuits had reduced Wade's inheritance, while disputes within his college meant he was in danger of losing his fellowship. Wade saw revealing the Bott affair to the Earl of Leicester as a way to secure a powerful patron. Eager for any weapon which would damage the Berkeleys, Leicester instructed Wade to collect evidence for him to put before the privy council. Wade confronted his uncle at his house in Coventry, terrifying other members of the family who as witnesses feared getting caught up in the affair. He then approached Bott, who demanded a pardon before he would make a confession. The puritan preacher Humphrey Fenn also became involved, offering to give evidence concerning what Phines, Bott and others had confessed to him about the affair. Bott was taken to London, where he was questioned by the clerk to the privy council and Robert Topcliffe, the notorious interrogator with a reputation for the use of torture. Faced with the possibility of being charged with having concealed treason, Bott backtracked. He now insisted the letter had concerned Leicester not the queen. Leicester died in September 1588, but the matter did not rest there, as the privy council encouraged Wade to continue his investigation.

This was an extremely difficult time for Katherine, who was well aware of Wade's investigation and the potential threat he posed. The rumours may explain why she did not attend the funeral of Mary, Queen of Scots in August 1587, despite having been expected to be among the leading mourners.[10] Then during the furore surrounding the Armada further charges were brought against Arundel, who was still languishing in the Tower, and he was condemned to death. The sentence was not carried out, but the earl eventually died still a prisoner in the Tower in 1595. Katherine's sister Jane, countess of Westmorland died in 1593 and was buried at Kenninghall, while her husband lived on in exile until 1601. Their daughters had all been raised as catholics. Following her mother's death, Margaret Neville was arrested along with her maid and a seminary priest in a raid on her house near Durham. Convicted, she spent some time in the custody of the Bishop of Durham and was eventually pardoned by the queen as a result of her 'pretended conformity'.[11] She subsequently reverted to catholicism. Her sister Katherine had been protected by the protestantism of her husband Sir Thomas Grey of Chillingham, Northumberland, until his death in 1590. Thereafter she eluded arrest for harbouring priests until 1598 by moving between rented houses. She was also released after a brief captivity and later allegedly maintained three houses for sheltering priests in London.

It seems doubtful that Katherine was ever in any real danger. As is apparent from the treatment of her nieces, her gender, status and kinship with the queen all helped to protect her. There is no evidence that she was ever directly questioned over the Bott affair. Although the council wrote to the leading gentry in Warwickshire asking them to help Wade with his legal disputes, their letter had little effect. Nor did the council prevent Magdalen College depriving him of his fellowship. The position of the college may well have been influenced by the Berkeleys' decision to send their son Thomas with his small retinue to study there. Since neither Leicester or his brother Warwick, who died in 1590, had produced an heir, their deaths disrupted the established political order in the Midlands. The council was reluctant to disturb it further by arresting Lord Berkeley's wife. It suited them to use Wade's investigation to persuade the Berkeleys to demonstrate their support for the established order. Accordingly the Archbishop of Canterbury wrote to Henry advising him that he and his wife would be wise to be seen attending church services with their entire household.

The privy council's investigation of Katherine, the problems of the Earl of Arundel, and the arrests of Katherine's nieces coincided with the breakdown of Mary Berkeley's marriage to John Zouch. Her father-in-law had died in 1585, leaving his son a heavily indebted estate. Although he was chosen as knight of the shire for Derbyshire in 1589, his worsening financial position meant John could not maintain his position within the county. He and Mary had two children, but John complained he had been 'ignorantly married to his mother'.[12] The couple separated and after a legal battle an income of £200 a year was secured for Mary. John's mother also had to fight her son to get the income from her jointure. To keep himself afloat John was forced to sell his ironworks and other land, although he retained the family seat at Codnor.

4 Careys and Townshends

By 1590 Thomas Berkeley, now a student at Oxford, was old enough to be legally married and his parents started to look for a suitable bride. The search became more urgent, when Thomas fell ill with a 'burning fever' after three years at Oxford.[1] The continuation of the barony, and the future of those whose fortunes were associated with it, depended on Thomas and his future male heirs. Moreover his mother's health was also deteriorating. She was suffering from dropsy and had such extreme pain in the joints of one hand that surgery was required. Given the choice of two operations, Lady Berkeley chose the more painful. She disdained to have her servants hold her still and went through the ordeal allegedly without blenching. Her worsening health spurred Katherine on to arrange Thomas's marriage, since she did not trust Henry to manage such an important undertaking.

The choice of bride fell on Elizabeth, the only child of Sir George Carey and granddaughter of Henry, lord Hunsdon. As the son of Anne Boleyn's sister Mary her grandfather was Elizabeth I's closest male relative. (Lettice, the dowager countess of Essex and Leicester was his niece.) He had been a gentleman of his royal cousin's household during Mary I's reign and raised to the peerage following her accession to the throne. His eldest daughter Katherine was a member of the queen's privy chamber from 1560, when she was fifteen. In 1563 Katherine had married Charles Howard, Lady Berkeley's cousin and former schoolfellow. In 1568 Lord Hunsdon was sent to the north of England, charged with protecting English interests in the turmoil created by the civil war in Scotland. He was governor of Berwick in 1569, but was absent when the earls of Westmorland and Northumberland rose against the queen. His eldest son George, Elizabeth's father, assisted him in the aftermath of the rising and was knighted for his military service in 1570, aged twenty-two. In 1584 one of Lord Hunsdon's younger daughters, Philadelphia, married Thomas, lord Scrope, the son of Lady Berkeley's sister Margaret.

In 1574 Sir George Carey married Elizabeth, daughter of Sir John Spencer of Althorp, Northamptonshire. The Spencer wealth, founded on sheep farming, was vast. It enabled Sir John to provide good settlements for all his four sons and six daughters, securing them spouses of a higher social rank than his own. At the time of his heir's marriage the queen made Lord Hunsdon keeper of Somerset House on the Strand. This became his base in London, while Sir George and his new wife took over the family's mansion in Blackfriars.

Elizabeth Carey was born in May 1576 at her grandfather's palatial house at Hunsdon, Hertfordshire. The original fifteenth-century brick house had been acquired by Henry VII and greatly expanded in the next reign. Henry VIII had visited frequently to hunt in its deer park, but the house was predominantly used as a residence for his children. It had been granted to Elizabeth's grandfather by the queen before his elevation to the peerage. Although Elizabeth was the only one of her parents' children to survive early infancy, her's was not a lonely childhood. Her grandparents had a large family and many of Elizabeth's cousins also spent time at Hunsdon. Elizabeth's education was overseen by her mother. Lady Carey was a patron of the poet Edmund Spenser, to whom she was distantly related. Thomas Nashe, the greatest of the Elizabethan pamphleteers, praised her piety, modesty and generosity to scholars. Various other authors dedicated works to her in gratitude for or hope of patronage. Lady Carey was herself well-educated and ensured that her daughter was similarly learned. Before her marriage Elizabeth was sufficiently skilled in Italian to translate two of Petrarch's sonnets with the help of her father's secretary Henry Stanford, who also acted as her tutor. A letter written by Stanford to Elizabeth some years after her marriage indicates her familiarity with classical and Renaissance literature.[2]

Elizabeth was brought up in close proximity to the court. When she was christened, the queen and Anne, countess of Warwick were her godmothers. Her aunt Katherine, lady Howard remained a prominent member of the queen's household. In 1577 Lord Hunsdon moved to the centre of power on his appointment to the privy council. The following year Elizabeth's father obtained his first court appointment as earl marshal and her mother became a member of the queen's privy chamber. Shortly after her maternal aunt Alice Spencer also joined the queen's household following her marriage to Ferdinand, lord Strange, heir of the Earl of Derby. As the great-grandson of Mary Tudor, Ferdinand was a close relative of the queen and had been a member of the royal household since he was fourteen. In 1585, when Elizabeth was nine, Lord Hunsdon was appointed lord chamberlain, the senior official responsible for organising court entertainments.

In addition to his court appointments Elizabeth's father had a number of military and civil roles that frequently took him away from the capital. A letter written to his wife during one of these absences, addressing her as his 'sweete pugge', suggests that the marriage was a close and affectionate one.[3] In 1583 Sir George Carey was appointed governor of the strategically important Isle of Wight. There he rebuilt the domestic buildings of Carisbrooke castle to make a dwelling fit for an Elizabethan magnate and became noted for his extravagant hospitality.

Although she had lived predominantly close to London and the court, Elizabeth also had Warwickshire connections through her mother's family. Her grandfather Sir John Spencer had settled an estate at Claverdon, near Stratford on Avon, on his son Thomas, while his daughter Katherine had married Sir Thomas Leigh of Stoneleigh, a dissolved abbey less than ten miles from Caludon. In 1572 Henry and Katherine had sold the manor of Thurlaston and their land in Dunchurch to Sir Thomas Leigh's widowed mother Alice. Once married, Elizabeth would have members of her own family within reach when she was in the country, and would not be dependent solely on her husband's family. Increasing the range of their kinship ties within the Midlands would also be useful to the Berkeleys in maintaining their status, helping to counteract the effect of their sales of land.

The Earl of Pembroke had sought Elizabeth as a bride for his own son and heir, but his terms were too steep for Sir George Carey. The Berkeleys were willing to accept a lower dowry. The negotiations of the marriage settlement required tact and caution, to ensure that securing a potentially wealthy prize did not come at too high a price. Katherine was also concerned that they should not become public knowledge. Once the Countess of Warwick knew the Careys were about to have a vested interest in the Berkeley lawsuit, she might well be anxious to reach a settlement before their influence could be brought to bear. Consequently Katherine took a leading role in the marriage negotiations, determined not to involve her husband until it was essential. She encouraged her servants and legal advisors to keep Henry away from London. By the autumn of 1595 an agreement in principle was reached. Lord Berkeley, now summoned to London by his wife, took Thomas to be formally introduced to Elizabeth at

Careys and Townshends

Blackfriars. The agreed marriage portion was £1,000 in cash and the settlement of land in Kent worth £1,000 a year to pass to Elizabeth after the death of both her parents. The bulk of the Hunsdon lands would pass to her uncle Sir John Carey, who as the male heir would inherit the title. In return it was agreed, that twenty-seven manors from Henry's remaining estate would be conveyed to trustees, to ensure they passed to the couple after Henry's death. This included sixteen manors in Gloucestershire, two in Somerset, four in Sussex, four in Leicestershire and Caludon in Warwickshire.

The wedding took place at Blackfriars in February 1596. Compared to the low key weddings of his father and grandfather, the marriage of Thomas Berkeley was celebrated in grand style with a high proportion of the court in attendance. Given Elizabeth's court connections and the familial relationship of both bride and groom to Elizabeth I, it may have been hoped that the queen herself would attend. However, since John Smyth does not mention the queen's presence, we can assume that she was not there. To assist with organising court entertainments Elizabeth's grandfather was the patron of the theatre group founded in 1594 to which Shakespeare belonged. The company, then known as the Lord Chamberlain's Men, had secured the lease of a property in Blackfriars for a theatre at the beginning of February 1596. Hence a tradition grew up that it was for the wedding of Thomas and Elizabeth at Blackfriars a fortnight later that *A Midsummer Night's Dream* was written and first performed.

Katherine, lady Berkeley died at Caludon in April 1596, less than two months after seeing her son successfully married. She was fifty-eight years old. Her funeral was used by the government as a further demonstration that the Berkeleys were part of a stable political order. The queen ordered that there should be a splendid heraldic funeral in St Michael's church, Coventry on Ascension Day. Such grand funerals invariably took several weeks to arrange, so the six week gap between Katherine's death and her burial was not unusual. Yet, by choosing an important feast day of the church for this grand spectacle in a provincial city with a strong puritan element, the queen and her council made maximum use of this opportunity for political theatre. Since protocol dictated that the chief mourner should be of the same sex as the deceased, this role was taken by Anne, eldest daughter of the late earl of Derby and first cousin of Katherine's young daughter-in-law. The sixteen-year-old Anne was supported by Katherine's son, his wife Elizabeth and Elizabeth's parents. The long procession was arranged in hierarchic order by the heralds and included the leaders of local gentry society, seventy-four of Henry's gentlemen, the officers of the Berkeley household, Katherine's own attendants and seventy poor women. After the service the whole company returned to Caludon for a feast, the remains of which were said to have fed a thousand poor people. A full description of the funeral was prepared for Henry. Denied the role of chief mourner by protocol, he had stayed behind in his own apartment, while his wife of over forty years was laid to rest.

That July Elizabeth's grandfather Lord Hunsdon died at Somerset House. He was given a magnificent funeral in Westminster Abbey, paid for by the usually parsimonious queen. The monument, subsequently erected by Elizabeth's father, is the largest in the abbey and covered with an immense display of heraldry. Lord Hunsdon had not prepared a will, but his deathbed wishes were recorded before witnesses. He hoped that Elizabeth's father would succeed not only to his title, but also to all his offices in accordance with the 'sundry gracious promises' he had received from the queen.[4] In the event Lord Cobham was appointed lord chamberlain, although the new Lord Hunsdon did succeed his father as captain of the gentlemen pensioners. The appointment of the sixty-nine-year-old Cobham, an experienced diplomat and councillor, was probably secured by his son-in-law Sir Robert Cecil. Cecil wanted to ensure that Cobham would remain in England, to shore up his support on the privy council against the rival faction led by the Earl of Essex. The lord chamberlain's duties required his attendance at court. So, once Cobham held that post, the Essex faction could not engineer his inclusion in a diplomatic mission overseas. When Cobham died the following year, Elizabeth's father did become lord chamberlain and a member of the privy council. He too supported the Cecil faction on the council against Essex.

The marriage of Thomas and Elizabeth quickly proved fruitful. Their daughter Theophila was born at Blackfriars on 11 December 1596. She was christened at the end of the year and had the queen and Essex as her godparents. Elizabeth and her husband had an annuity of £600, on which they found it impossible to maintain the expensive lifestyle necessitated by attendance at court. Like Thomas's parents before them, they quickly began accumulating debts and regularly spent more than three times their income. Moreover, Sir Thomas rapidly lost interest in domestic life. After Theophila's birth there were no more successful pregnancies for several years, and the marriage began to be troubled.

Meanwhile Lord Berkeley, after forty years of marriage to a stronger partner, seems to have been somewhat adrift without a wife and quickly began looking for a replacement. Another marriage also held out the prospect of improving his finances. Initially he appears to have set his sights high. Ferdinand, lord Strange had succeeded his father as Earl of Derby in 1593. Seven months later he was dead, allegedly poisoned by Jesuits for revealing a catholic plot against the queen. This had left his wife Alice, aunt to Henry's daughter-in-law, as an extremely eligible widow. Attempting to woo the dowager countess, Henry gave her an expensive mother-of-pearl lute, which had belonged to Katherine and, according to Smyth, in his 'widowers freedom' called her mistress. However, as Ferdinand and Alice had three daughters but no sons, the title went to his younger brother and the family became engaged in a legal dispute over the respective rights of the widow, her daughters and the male heir. Marriage to the impoverished Lord Berkeley would not have materially benefitted Alice. When she eventually remarried, it was to the eminent lawyer Sir Thomas Egerton, who as lord keeper was well placed to help her case. Realizing he had no hope of successfully wooing Alice, Henry turned his attention to one of her gentlewomen, coming close to marrying 'Mrs Ratcliffe'. This was probably Jane, daughter of Sir John Radcliffe of Ordsall, Lancashire, who was in her early twenties.[5]

The prospect of Henry marrying a young, nubile, but not particularly wealthy wife with a very real prospect of producing more children would have been unwelcome to his son and daughter-in-law. It was in their interest to encourage him to chose a wife nearer his own age. Then in 1597 a suspected Irish spy was arrested in Nuneaton, who the local schoolmaster claimed had been seeking Henry's help. The subsequent investigation into the affair by the privy council brought Henry into 'some trouble and danger'.[6] This was not the ideal time to think of marrying a young bride from notoriously catholic Lancashire. A matronly protestant wife was a far safer prospect and the ideal candidate was available within his immediate circle. Jane Townshend, wife of Roger, who Henry had known for three decades, had been a widow since 1590. In March 1598 Henry married Jane at St Giles without Cripplegate, close to her London house at the Barbican.

~~~

Like her predecessor Jane's early life had been overshadowed by the violence of Tudor politics. Her father Sir Michael Stanhope was born into a leading Nottinghamshire family. In Henry VIII's reign his half-sister married Edward Seymour, uncle of Edward VI. This connection led Sir Michael into a career in royal service, and as groom of the stole he became one of the inner circle around the young king. He was also keeper of the royal park at Beddington, near the palace of Nonsuch in Surrey and it was in the newly-built house at Beddington that he and his family lived during these years. When Seymour was ousted from power by the Duke of Northumberland, his brother-in-law was arrested and imprisoned in the Tower. Sir Michael was executed in February 1552, leaving his wife Anne to bring up his five young sons and three daughters.

The family were not made destitute by the conviction and execution of Jane's father, as much of their land was entailed and Sir Michael had prudently increased his wife's jointure during the months of factional tension preceding Seymour's eventual fall. When Mary I came to the throne, their situation improved further as the queen was sympathetic to those who had suffered under Northumberland's rule. The family settled at Shelford, a former priory in the south of Nottinghamshire that her father had acquired fifteen years before. There Jane was raised in a pious, protestant household. As a child she observed how successfully her determined mother managed the family's affairs during her widowhood, consolidating and extending the scattered Stanhope estate. Anne's efforts meant that her eldest son succeeded to a more manageable estate than that left by his father, which was easier to exploit and so maximise his income. Anne Stanhope also showed a particular interest in the value of education. All four of her younger sons were sent to Cambridge and then on to Gray's Inn to study the common law and to take advantage of the other opportunities London presented. While two followed careers as courtiers, another became a common lawyer and member of the

Council of the North, and the fourth an ecclesiastical lawyer. All five of Jane's brothers were active men of affairs who served as MPs. Jane and her sisters were taught at home. In keeping with the aristocratic and courtly milieu in which their parents had moved, they were taught languages, music and other accomplishments as well as such practical skills as casting accounts.

Jane married Roger Townshend, when she was eighteen. This was a far grander match than those arranged for her two elder sisters. As a child Roger had inherited a considerable estate in Norfolk and Suffolk from his great-grandfather and as a young man had married the daughter of one of his Norfolk neighbours. He presumably met Jane through her brothers, either while a student at Cambridge or later in London. Left a childless widower by the death of his first wife, he offered Jane an unusually large jointure as part of the marriage agreement. This suggests a love match, with Roger determined to secure Jane by offering her a very generous settlement. Although he was a wealthy landowner in his own right, Roger had followed his great-grandfather into the service of the Howards. As Norfolk's and later Arundel's man-of-business he spent much of his time in London rather than on his own estates. Jane too seems to have lived predominantly in the capital. Over the years she had got to know Lord Berkeley and his wife well.

The period of the arrest, trial and execution of the Duke of Norfolk had been an anxious time for Jane, fearing that her husband might himself be implicated in the duke's alleged treason. In the event Roger emerged unscathed from the experience. Later, when he took charge of the affairs of the duke's heir, he and Jane also drew closer to the court and both appear among those giving New Year's gifts to the queen. The couple were apparently regarded as a positive protestant influence on the Earl of Arundel. When Arundel was himself imprisoned in 1585, Roger was temporarily taken in to custody. He was soon released and there were clearly no doubts about his loyalty to the queen. Although his service to the Howards drew mainly on his legal training and financial acumen, Roger also had the martial training appropriate to an Elizabethan courtier. In 1588 he played his part in the defence of the country against the Armada and in reward was knighted at sea by Charles, lord Howard.

Jane and Roger had various children, but only two sons survived childhood. When Sir Roger died in 1590, the elder John was just of age and the younger Roger was ten. As a result of her generous marriage settlement, Jane became a wealthy widow with an income of around £1,000 a year. While John inherited a substantial estate from his father, its immediate value was significantly reduced by his mother's life interest. Robert was left what his parents believed would enable him to maintain himself as a gentleman, provided he was not extravagant. His inheritance too was affected by his mother's life interest. Her control of a large part of the Townshend estate gave Jane considerable influence over her sons.[7]

Like many young courtiers John Townshend gained military experience fighting under Sir Francis Vere in the Low Countries in 1592. The following year he married Anne, one of the three daughters of Sir Nathaniel Bacon of Stiffkey. The marriage was both financially lucrative and brought connection to a family that was locally important and linked to the court. Anne's grandfather Sir Nicholas Bacon had been Elizabeth I's lord keeper and the philosopher Sir Francis Bacon was her uncle. Within months of the marriage Anne's mother died. John then began a bitter dispute with his father-in-law over the terms of the marriage settlement. John was worried that, if Sir Nathaniel remarried and produced a son, Anne would inherit less than expected from her father. Although John's stance was not unusual, the dispute arising so soon after her marriage placed Anne in a difficult position and was one source of strain on the marriage. Another was the difference in background between the couple. John was accustomed to the sophisticated atmosphere of London and the court, while Anne had led a very sheltered life in Norfolk. In 1596 John took part in the Cadiz expedition, during which he was knighted. Although he was involved in the local politics of Norfolk, he spent much of his time at court. While encumbered by his mother's life interest, his estate was insufficient to sustain his extravagant lifestyle. This placed a further strain on his marriage. The couple never seem to have overcome their early difficulties, although they did manage to produce three children.

When Lord Berkeley wed Jane Townshend it was very much a marriage of convenience, which may not have been consummated. Jane continued to live predominantly at the Barbican, while Henry remained in Warwickshire. Their servants maintained that the couple never shared a bed, although Henry would stay at the Barbican house when in London. Smyth referred to 'this amorous humour or dotage in old men' that led them to marry, when it was not for procreation, the avoidance of fornication or mutual society, help and comfort, but politically the marriage was an astute move for Henry.[8] Jane's protestantism helped to distance him from his catholic associations and cemented his links with the court. With her brother's help Jane had negotiated another generous settlement for herself, securing the promise of £300 a year during Henry's life and a jointure of £1,000 a year after his death. The guarantors of Jane's settlement included her brother Sir Michael Stanhope and Thomas Howard, Arundel's younger brother.

The social hierarchy of Elizabethan England was marked by very precise gradations and her marriage to Henry provided Jane with a significant step up in status. This is demonstrated by the different ways in which her elder brother Edward referred to Jane and his sisters-in-law in his will, written in 1603. Margaret, the wife of his courtier brother Sir John Stanhope is referred to as 'my honourable sister' and two other sisters-in-law as 'loving' sisters, but Jane, lady Berkeley, is 'my very honourable lady and sister'.[9] Although such formality is alien to modern society, particularly within the confines of the family, it was very real and significant in Elizabethan England and would have affected Jane in various practical ways. She would have been expected to keep a larger household than the wife or widow of a knight, to have more servants and to observe a greater formality. She could expect to receive deference from those below her in the social hierarchy, but also to receive a correspondingly larger volume of requests for patronage.

When Henry failed to fulfil his side of their marriage settlement, Jane insisted her trustees took action against him. In an apparent attempt to reduce his outgoings, Henry went to stay at Newnham Paddox to the east of Coventry. Basil Feilding, the owner of Newnham Paddox, and his wife were among the local gentry who had taken part in Katherine's funeral procession. Henry's attempts to save money proved insufficient. Two years after his marriage to Jane, he was forced to sell his lands in Huntingdonshire to raise £4,000 as a cash settlement for his wife's outstanding claims. Despite this dispute Henry and Jane remained on friendly terms, her house at the Barbican continuing to provide him with a useful base when he visited London.

Both Jane's sons lived as spendthrift courtiers rather than settling down to the more frugal lifestyle of country squires, which their restricted incomes would have supported. The younger son Robert had followed his brother's swashbuckling ways and earned himself a knighthood. Such titles brought with them expectations of conspicuous consumption and patronage, but no money to support them. When her sons' debts became insurmountable, Jane was forced to act. She bought two manors in Norfolk from John and three in Essex from Robert to prevent them being sold outside the family. Since it was the generosity of her own marriage settlement that kept her sons comparatively impoverished, this was the least they might expect her to do. It meant that the reins of power within the family were firmly held by Jane rather than John, its nominal head. He was forced to rely on her to return the purchased manors to the Townshend estate in her will. John was hot-headed and prone to settle his quarrels through violence. Such intemperance was not unusual among the Elizabethan gentry, but John had the additional frustration of his financial dependence on his mother and an unhappy marriage. In 1600 it took the intervention of the privy council to prevent him fighting a duel. Duelling was a scourge of Elizabeth's court, where young men would react to perceived insults to their honour by fighting. John's kinsman by marriage, Sir Francis Bacon would later describe it as a desperate evil, caused by a sorcery that bewitched the young.

In early 1601 Elizabeth Berkeley realised that she was again pregnant. Around the same time Thomas left England for an extended tour of Europe, possibly to escape the consequences of having sold some of his interest in Berkeley properties without his father's consent. Although foreign travel was considered a useful part of a young aristocrat's education, it was something that was usually undertaken before or immediately after marriage. It was also considered preferable to travel as part of an official embassy. Independent travel by a young man with family responsibilities was considered reprehensible. Where a family had catholic associations like the Berkeleys, it was also liable to be viewed with suspicion. Meanwhile, since they had established no home of their own, Elizabeth was left to stay with family members or to rent accommodation for herself and their child. In October 1601 she was living at Leyton, five miles outside the capital on the road to Epping Forest, when their son George was born. His christening was a far more subdued affair than that of his sister. His godparents were his grandfather Hunsdon, step-grandmother Jane, and Charles Howard, now earl of Nottingham.

~~~

When Elizabeth I died in March 1603, Thomas Berkeley was part of the official delegation that hurried to Scotland to tell James I that he had been proclaimed king. His wife was among the ladies, who followed at a more dignified pace. The official delegation arrived to find that they had been beaten by Elizabeth's uncle Sir Robert Carey, who rode non-stop from Richmond Palace to Holyrood as soon as he received confirmation of the queen's death. As Elizabeth I's cousin, Carey knew his status would inevitably suffer after her death, as he had no familial tie to her successor. While his haste was censured by the privy council as disrespectful to the queen's memory, it ensured that he secured the king's notice. In his initial euphoria the king made Carey a gentleman of the bedchamber, although his English council subsequently persuaded James to demote him to the less intimate office of gentleman of the privy chamber. Carey's wife was meanwhile given charge of the king's younger son, who would eventually succeed him as Charles I. This ensured that the benefits of Carey's prompt action continued into the following reign. As a member of the official delegation Thomas had to be satisfied with following in the family tradition by being made a knight of the bath at the coronation. He was also chosen as one of Gloucestershire's two representatives in the first Jacobean parliament. He did not receive, as he must have hoped, an office at court that would have helped ease his financial position. Thomas's brother-in-law John Zouch, who had retained Codnor castle despite his debts, was among the Derbyshire gentlemen knighted by the king as he made his leisurely way from Scotland to England. Lord Berkeley meanwhile was appointed to the lord lieutenancy of Gloucestershire.

While her uncle succeeded in securing his position at court, Elizabeth's father was effectively eclipsed by the queen's death. Lord Hunsdon had been suffering ill-health for some time and had made his will in the spring of 1599.[10] In 1602 he spent the summer taking the waters at Bath. At the end of that year Katherine's nephew Thomas Howard was appointed as acting lord chamberlain in his place. Following the accession of James I, Hunsdon was relieved of his office. He died four months later and was succeeded as Lord Hunsdon by his younger brother John, who played little part in court life. While the status of Elizabeth's family was reduced, the stock of her husband's Howard relatives grew. His uncle Henry had been in contact with the Scottish king from 1598 and had collaborated with Sir Robert Cecil to ensure a smooth transition. He was appointed to the privy council along with his son in May 1603 and the following spring was created Earl of Northampton. He was also one of the five principal commissioners appointed to negotiate peace with Spain. Katherine's nephew Thomas was confirmed as lord chamberlain and became Earl of Suffolk at the coronation

In the summer of 1603 a quarrel with Sir Matthew Browne led Jane Berkeley's son Sir John Townshend into another duel. This time there was no intervention from the privy council to prevent it. The two opponents were similar in age and married with young families. They were both associated with the Earl of Nottingham and had earned their knighthoods at Cadiz. They fought on Hounslow Heath. Browne was killed outright. John was wounded and died the following day. His elder son Roger was just eight years old. Jane purchased Roger's wardship for £4,000, which gave her control of his estate and the right to arrange his marriage. This further cemented Jane's position as matriarch, with a legal power over her grandchildren exceeding that of their mother. As a widow Jane's daughter-in-law Anne lived quietly at Heydon, north of Norwich on the restricted income provided by her jointure. Important decisions concerning her children were taken by her mother-in-law and her father with little reference to her own views. In 1602 Jane had begun building a house in Walton-on-Thames, Surrey. She may have intended this to be used by her son, when the king was at Hampton Court, as it was sold after John's death. Jane then purchased a house at Kensington, a fashionable area outside the city popular for its clean air.

If Sir Thomas Berkeley and his wife had hoped her father would ease their immediate financial worries through his will, they were disappointed. As expected, Elizabeth was left land in addition to that which had been settled on her at her marriage. In time she would receive the house at Blackfriars and other property in Middlesex, Suffolk and the Isle of Wight, but only once her mother had died. In the meantime Elizabeth and Thomas still had only their annuity on which to live and it was proving increasingly inadequate. They continued to spend more than three times their income each year. The only recourse was to sell parts of their inheritance, before it had even passed fully into their hands. In 1606 detailed accounts of their debts were drawn up and this time Lord Berkeley and Smyth, as his man-of-business, were involved in the negotiations for the necessary sales. Elizabeth was also actively involved and expressed decided views over which assets should be realised and which retained.[11] Much of her interest in land in Kent, which she had brought to the marriage, was sacrificed to pay the debts. Once it was all over, Thomas again left the country. It was probably intended that, living abroad, he would spend less than attending the court. Yet he continued to run up debts as he travelled through France and into Italy. By visiting these catholic countries, he also risked arousing suspicions about the religious opinions he had learnt at his mother's knee.

The changes at court following the accession of James I helped Lord Berkeley to finally settle the lawsuit, which had dragged on throughout Elizabeth's reign. Anne, countess of Warwick, with whom he had been unable to reach a settlement, died in 1604. The claim to the disputed property was inherited by Robert Sidney, the younger of the two brothers that Katherine had rejected as potential sons-in-law more than thirty years before. Sidney was also in favour with the king, having been made lord chamberlain of the queen's household and ennobled as Viscount Lisle. Lord Lisle wished to live in aristocratic style and had ambitions to rise higher in the peerage. It was, therefore, in his interest to come to a settlement with Lord Berkeley, which would bring him a lump sum in compensation and free him from an expensive and interminable lawsuit. The negotiations took several years to conclude, but were eventually resolved by December 1609. Their lawyers had achieved a satisfactory settlement for the Berkeleys, but it required further disposals of land to raise Lord Lisle's compensation. This combined with his mounting debts brought Thomas back to England. By this stage his marriage had almost completely broken down. Elizabeth's letters to Smyth in this period were so frank, that she hoped he would burn them as she did his

Wives of the Berkeleys

replies. Eventually an agreement was drawn up to reduce Thomas's expenditure and to hand financial control of his affairs to his wife and Smyth. References in the agreement to the drunken, disorderly members of his household indicate the source of some of the disagreements between the pious, sensible Elizabeth and her husband. Just over a week later everything was ready for the couple to spend Christmas in Gloucestershire, where there was to be a formal ceremony to mark the ending of the lawsuit. Then Thomas and Elizabeth had a row. He stormed out, announced his intention to go abroad and ordered Elizabeth to move at once to her uncle's house at Claverdon. In a furious letter Smyth defended Elizabeth, pointed out some home truths to Thomas, and refused to assist his flight. Things were patched up sufficiently to get them through Christmas and its ceremonies, but Thomas left for France immediately afterwards.[12]

Having spent a year travelling through France and Italy, Thomas returned north into the Low Countries. There a messenger from Elizabeth managed to find him and persuade Thomas to return to England in the summer of 1611. The couple were reconciled and Elizabeth became pregnant once more, but Thomas's always delicate health had deteriorated. He spent part of the summer at Berkeley castle with his father. When he showed no signs of rallying, Thomas was moved to Smyth's house at North Nibley, the air on the side of the Cotswold escarpment being thought healthier than that close to the river. At the end of September Elizabeth and Henry moved Thomas to Caludon castle, where he died aged thirty-six towards the end of November. A son was born after Thomas had died, but lived only a few weeks. This was the fifth child that Elizabeth had borne and seen die. Both father and son were buried with Thomas's mother in Coventry.

As Elizabeth mourned the death of her husband and baby son, her mother was negotiating a second marriage. The dowager Lady Hunsdon was a temptingly wealthy widow, whose position was bolstered by being the executrix of her husband's will. Towards the end of 1612 she married Ralph, lord Eure, a comparatively impoverished northern baron and recent widower. The couple had known each other for many years, from the time when Elizabeth's father and grandfather had been based in the north of England. It appears to have been a political marriage. Eure had been appointed president of the Council of Wales in 1607, at a time when the gentry of the English border counties were challenging its jurisdiction. Marriage to a wealthy woman who was allied through her daughter's marriage to the Berkeleys, one of the leading families in the region, helped to bolster Eure's position during his last years on the council. His new wife's house in Blackfriars also provided him with a convenient base in London. Unlike her predecessor it is unlikely that the new Lady Eure ever ventured to Ludlow.

When Thomas Berkeley died, his daughter Theophila was a month short of her fifteenth birthday and his son George was just ten. Theophila was the same age as the king's eldest daughter, who spent her childhood in England at Coombe Abbey within a few miles of Caludon. Theophila was conveniently placed to become a companion of the young princess and share her lessons. Both girls were given an extensive education and developed a similarly serious, pious, literary outlook. In keeping with Elizabeth's belief in the importance of education, George was sent to school in Coventry, where he was taught by the translator Philemon Holland. The school had a good reputation and the city was known for its radical piety, which counteracted the suspicion of catholicism which had been rekindled by his father's travels. With Caludon being so close to the city, Elizabeth was also able to closely monitor her son while he was at the school.

5 Cokes and Stanhopes

When Princess Elizabeth married Frederick of Bohemia in February 1613, her former schoolfellow Theophila Berkeley was at the centre of the celebrations as one of the bridesmaids. Although the death of the king's elder son Prince Henry a few months before had cast a shadow over the court, the marriage of the young princess was celebrated in great style with fireworks, a mock sea battle, processions and masques. It all provided an excellent platform for Lady Berkeley to launch her daughter onto the marriage market. Within two months John Smyth was engaged in serious negotiations for a marriage between Theophila and Robert, eldest son of the jurist Sir Edward Coke. The negotiations took four months, during which time Smyth was working predominantly under Elizabeth's instructions. The couple were married at Berkeley in August 1613. Lord Berkeley expressed himself very happy with his grand-daughter's match, but one suspects his former wife would have viewed a connection to the Cokes as demeaning.

Sir Edward Coke was an ambitious man whose rise to influence and fortune resulted from a combination of an acute legal mind, powerful ambition and the ruthless exploitation of his opportunities. He himself had married well. His first wife Bridget Paston brought him a connection to one of the leading gentry families in Norfolk. They had ten children, of whom five sons and two daughters survived into adulthood. When Bridget died in 1598, Coke quickly remarried. His second wife Elizabeth, the daughter of Thomas Cecil, earl of Exeter and widow of Sir William Hatton, was a young, rich, society beauty. According to John Chamberlain, contemporaries were surprised 'that after so many large and likely offers' Elizabeth accepted Coke.[1] Although he was a rich and successful lawyer, who then held the office of attorney general, Coke's status was considerably below that of his bride. As a symbol of this difference Elizabeth continued to be called Lady Hatton after her second marriage. Gossip attributed the hasty wedding, which took place without ceremony at night, to Lady Hatton being pregnant by someone else. The birth of their first child precisely nine months after the wedding makes that highly unlikely. A more prosaic explanation is that Lady Hatton and her family recognised the advantage of securing by marriage the services of the leading lawyer of the age. Her first husband had been the heir of Sir Christopher Hatton, the former lord chancellor. Realising this inheritance had been complicated, because his uncle had died in debt to the crown. Coke proved useful in protecting the interests of Elizabeth and her stepdaughter against the competing claims of the crown and Sir William's male heir. Sir Robert Cecil may also have encouraged his niece's marriage for political reasons, as Coke was useful as an ally in the factional divisions at court. After the marriage Coke and his wife clashed over the way in which his interests took precedence over hers. A strong, intelligent and independent woman, she resented Coke's assumption of control over her property. Lady Hatton's powerlessness to resist her husband's decisions demonstrates the value of Jane Townshend's insistence on retaining control of her property on marriage to Lord Berkeley. Lady Hatton's second marriage produced two daughters, but was always tempestuous.

Sir Robert Coke was twenty-six, nine years older than Theophila. He had spent his early life within a quiet family circle at Huntingfield, Suffolk, presided over by his mother while his father pursued his legal career. After her death his life had been less settled. He was admitted to the Inner Temple in 1606, but was destined for the life of a landed gentleman rather than a career in the law. He was knighted the following year and thereafter lived on the periphery of the court until his marriage.

Theophila's grandfather had agreed to settle £3,000 on her, but this was insufficient to secure the Coke marriage. He also had to hand over the manor of Portbury, Somerset, worth £8,000. Initially the couple lived at Caludon and Sir Robert sat for Coventry in the parliament of 1614. Like Theophila's parents before them, they suffered from the problem of having an expectation of great wealth in the future while living on a small income in the interim. They too built up significant debts, although Sir Robert's vice was avid book-collecting rather than the drinking and restless travel that had absorbed Sir Thomas Berkeley. The couple were well-suited and, despite the strain of their early money worries and a lack of children, the marriage appears to have been happy.

Three months after Theophila's marriage, her grandfather died at Caludon. The body was carried back to Berkeley for burial in the family chapel. When Sir Thomas had died, it had become apparent that Lord Henry was likely to die before the new heir George was of age. The Berkeleys were greatly concerned about the damage that could be done to an estate during a minority. Elizabeth had the additional personal concern that her son might be taken out of her care and his marriage arranged without her agreement. Accordingly, before his death Henry had approached his brother-in-law Henry Howard, now earl of Northampton and prominent at court, and asked him to secure the wardship and to allow Elizabeth to raise George herself. It was even hoped that the childless Northampton might make George his heir and thus repair some of the losses endured by the Berkeley estates in recent years. Northampton did as requested and acquired the wardship. George was removed from school in Coventry and taken to London by his mother, where the 'sober and vertuous' Oxford graduate Henry Ashwood was employed as his tutor.[2]

The parlous state of the Berkeley finances at this time meant that the only speedy solution was to marry George, the new lord Berkeley, to a wealthy heiress. Conveniently, his step-grandmother Jane had a niece, who would inherit a share of two estates. This niece, Elizabeth, was the nine-year-old daughter of Jane's brother Sir Michael Stanhope. Sir Michael had married late in life, when he was already in his sixties. His career as a courtier had not been particularly impressive, but he eventually rose to be a gentleman of the bedchamber. The grant of a monopoly on importing Spanish wool for felt hats had enabled him to establish a modest fortune and purchase an estate at Sudbourne, Suffolk. His wife Anne was the daughter of Sir William Reade of Osterley, Middlesex. The son of a London mercer, Sir William had inherited much of the fortune of his step-father, the merchant and financier Sir Thomas Gresham, founder of the Royal Exchange. Anne was about thirty years younger than her husband. Her father's fortune had enabled him to marry his elder son Thomas to Mildred Cecil, daughter of the Earl of Exeter and sister to Lady Hatton. This brother died childless shortly before Anne's marriage. Her younger brother Francis had married Elizabeth, the daughter and co-heiress of Thomas, lord Burgh and widow of George Brooke, a younger son of Lord Cobham. Her first husband, with whom she had three children, had been involved in a conspiracy against James I and executed in December 1603. During the investigation of the plot, it became public knowledge that Brooke had seduced his wife's younger sister. Elizabeth Burgh enjoyed no greater success in her marriage to Francis Reade. Very soon after the wedding Francis became involved in a violent incident, which resulted in his prosecution for manslaughter. He was convicted and, despite the best efforts of his extended family to secure him a pardon, spent the rest of his life in prison. Since neither of her brothers had produced an heir, Anne Stanhope and her daughters became the heirs presumptive to her father's considerable fortune. Following the death of his first wife in 1605, Sir William remarried a much younger woman in an apparent attempt to produce a male heir, but he had no further children.

Sir Michael was willing to settle the reversion of property worth £1,500 a year on his daughter and it was reasonably expected that she would inherit a similar amount from her grandfather. Her father also undertook to settle on Elizabeth his house in St John's Lane, Clerkenwell, a fashionable part of London close to the Barbican. This ensured the couple would have somewhere to live in London. This was a sizeable prospective fortune, which would to an extent compensate for the dissipation of the Berkeley estate under George's father and grandfather. The previous year a similar settlement had seen Elizabeth's sister Jane married to Henry, viscount Fitzwalter, the elder son of the Earl of Sussex. Negotiations for George's marriage proceeded with the approval of Northampton, as George's legal guardian. The close relationship that developed between George's mother and Sir Michael as a result of their children's marriage is suggested by his later leaving her a diamond ring in his will.[3]

Northampton died a few months after George's marriage. In the event his gratitude for the support he had received from his sister Katherine during her life proved to have a severely limited influence. In his will he assigned George's wardship to Elizabeth's uncles Sir Richard and Sir Thomas Spencer, on condition that £1,500 was paid to his estate for the same. This, he claimed, was roughly what it had cost him. The bulk of Northampton's large estate passed to his great-nephew the Earl of Arundel, while his nephew the Earl of Suffolk acquired his house in Charing Cross.[4] Although Elizabeth and Sir Michael Stanhope attempted to avoid paying for the wardship, they were eventually forced to settle.

The marriage between Elizabeth Stanhope and George Berkeley

took place at Easter 1614. The bride then returned to live with her parents. All was not happy in the Clerkenwell household. Her mother Anne, who was growing tired of her gout-ridden elderly husband, had taken a lover, reputed to be Sir Eustace Hart. In 1605 Hart had married Mary, the daughter of the Earl of Oxford and widow of Peregrine Bertie, lord Willoughby de Eresby, one of Elizabeth's leading generals and a neighbour of Jane Berkeley at the Barbican. Mary had six children by her first marriage, all of whom were under age at Lord Willoughby's death in 1601. In the last decade of his life ill-health had prevented Willoughby pursuing his active military career, which seems to have placed a strain on the marriage and the couple separated. Mary de Vere's second marriage to Hart was also troubled and there were periods of separation and reconciliation. It was during one of these separations that Hart apparently began an affair with Anne Stanhope. In 1615 Anne became pregnant. She gave birth to a daughter, Bridget, and died shortly after in April 1616. In July Hart obtained a pardon from the king for his adulteries, fuelling the rumour that he was Bridget's father. Although deaths following childbirth were not uncommon, the open scandal surrounding Bridget's birth meant that rumours inevitably circulated suggesting Anne had been poisoned by her enraged husband. While many children lost their parents at a young age, Elizabeth and her sister did so under particularly unsettling circumstances. Bridget was not recognised by Sir Michael, who sent her away to be raised in the country. When he came to write his will, he left none of his property to Bridget. She was not mentioned in the main body of the will, but in a codicil Sir Michael acknowledged her right to a third share in the Reade inheritance through her mother. Hart's wife died in 1624. Although he married a second time, he had no legitimate children. He died in 1634. Bridget was not mentioned in his will.[5]

~~~

When her grandson Roger came of age in 1616, Jane Berkeley still controlled much of the Townshend estate through her marriage settlement and the manors she had bought from her sons. The meagre inheritance from his father was burdened by his mother's jointure and the need to make provision for his two younger siblings. Roger also inherited the small estate left by his uncle Roger, who had died childless the previous year. Jane had ensured that her two grandsons were well-educated. In 1611 Roger was sent to Cambridge, where his tutor was the puritan divine Giles Fletcher, chosen by his grandfather Sir Nathaniel Bacon with Jane's full approval. Three years later he completed his education, as his Stanhope great-uncles had before him, with a spell at Gray's Inn. His younger brother Stanhope, named in honour of Jane's family, similarly followed Roger to Cambridge and Gray's Inn. Since James I pursued a policy of maintaining peace with his neighbours, the opportunities for gentlemen to earn a knighthood in battle like Roger's father, uncle and grandfather had dried up. So, in 1617 Jane paid for her grandson to become a baronet. This gave him the title and status that was appropriate to his prospects. It seems somewhat surprising that Jane did not arrange a marriage for Roger before he came of age. It was not unusual for children to be betrothed at a very early age and married by the time they reached puberty, as her niece Elizabeth and George Berkeley had been. As Roger and Stanhope were the only male representatives of the next generation of Townshends, it would have been usual for Roger at least to have been married young in an attempt to secure the succession. It may well be that Jane was not willing to sacrifice her own interests and make a sufficient immediate settlement of land and money on her grandson to satisfy a potential father-in-law.

Sir John Townshend's daughter Anne seems to have inherited some of her grandmother's determination and consequently to have earned Jane's respect. Anne fell in love with John Spelman, a close friend of her brother Roger and the son of a Norfolk landowner. In most respects it was a suitable match, but as John's father was still very much alive and had a number of other children to settle, Anne's family in Norfolk disapproved. They suspected John's father would use the money Anne brought to the marriage to finance settlements for his other children. Denied their approval, Anne apparently turned to her grandmother for help. Jane did nothing immediately, but in her carefully considered will she left Anne £2,000 to be paid to her at the age of 24 or within a year of her marriage, which ever occurred first.[6] There was no proviso, as was usual, that she should marry with the approval of her family and friends. Consequently, when Jane died in January 1618, the way was cleared for Anne to marry John. Her family seem to have tried to prevent this, by having Jane's steward depose that she regretted leaving the money without proviso and that she would have changed her will had she lived longer.[7] No use appears to have been made of the deposition. Presumably the lawyers thought it unlikely that they could convince anyone that Jane Berkeley had not known her own mind. Anne and John were married within the year.

The elder Lady Elizabeth Berkeley's mother Lady Eure also died early in 1618. Both Lady Eure and Jane Berkeley chose to be buried alongside their first husbands, the fathers of their children. The death of her mother meant that Elizabeth finally acquired the estate settled on her at her marriage and by her father's will, less the land which she had agreed should be sacrificed to settle her husband's debts. She was now a wealthy widow with a house at Blackfriars convenient for the court. She was also in a position to purchase a house and land at Cranford, Middlesex, twelve miles from the centre of London. There she established a large library containing thousands of books. Finally she bought Durdans, a house with a twelve acre park at Epsom, Surrey for Theophila and her husband. This was close to the royal palace of Nonsuch, which provided successive Stuart queens with a place of retreat from the formality of Whitehall. Ownership of Durdans would be transferred to Theophila, once Sir Robert inherited his estate on his father's death. George meanwhile proceeded to Christchurch, Oxford to complete his education, while his young wife presumably remained living with her father in London. Certainly both George and his wife were in London in the spring of 1619, when they took part in Anne of Denmark's funeral procession.

After over a decade of widowhood and with her son coming of age the elder Lady Berkeley married for a second time in 1622. The bridegroom was Sir Thomas Chamberlain, a judge of the court of King's Bench, who earlier in his career had acted as a solicitor for the Berkeleys. He was a widower around fifteen years older than Elizabeth, although as he had married late the four children from his first marriage were still young. The marriage settlement Elizabeth demanded would have gained the admiration of her former stepmother-in-law and of the unfortunate Lady Hatton. She insisted on retaining legal control of her own estate, while expecting an immediate payment of £1,000 and a similar amount each year should Sir Thomas die. She would live with her husband or in her own houses as she wished, not as he commanded. She also sought the power to demand to see the accounts of her husband's clerk and to purchase land and property on behalf of their unborn children.[8] (Since Elizabeth was in her late forties, there was little chance of the couple having children.) Outwardly it appears that Sir Thomas paid dearly for a marriage that brought him little benefit. Certainly this is what some of his contemporaries thought. When Sir Thomas died three years later, one of his fellow judges recorded in his diary that he had been unfortunate in a marriage for which he had paid £5,000.[9] However, as his eldest son was only eight in 1622, Sir Thomas was almost certainly motivated by thoughts of the future security of his children. Elizabeth had proved herself to be an effective and determined manager of her own and her children's affairs. Sir Thomas had known her over many years and shared her strongly protestant religious views. In his will Sir Thomas requested that the wardship of his heir should be granted to Elizabeth and four male executors, to whom the care of his three younger children was also entrusted.[10] He knew Elizabeth would ensure that his children were well-educated and fitted for the society into which she could introduce them. It was a short but very practical marriage.

The younger Lady Berkeley's grandfather Sir William Reade died in the autumn of 1621 and her father a few months later. Once George came of age in the following year, his mother's role as manager of George's estates was officially over and she retired to Cranford among her books. George had been in Paris, but returned to England and began living with his wife. Their first son was born in 1623, when Elizabeth was eighteen, and christened Charles. Two more children quickly followed: Elizabeth in 1624 and George two years later. From an early stage the marriage was troubled. Given her early experiences, Elizabeth was naturally insecure and, when pregnant with her third child, was described as almost mad from jealousy. She worried that George was keeping unsuitable company, getting into debt, and drinking too much. Anthony Stafford, an author to whom George acted as a patron and who had travelled with him in France, appealed to George's mother to visit and remonstrate with him.[11] To his mother it must all have seemed painfully familiar. Like his father before him, George took refuge from his problems by going on a foreign tour in 1626, leaving Elizabeth to give birth to their second son without his support. His travels lasted three years and took him far south into Italy. While he ran up further debts, he relied on his mother and his wife to manage his affairs at home.

Viscount Fitzwalter had died in 1620, leaving the younger Lady Berkeley's sister Jane a childless widow of nineteen. In the spring of 1621 Jane married Sir William Withypoll of Ipswich, Suffolk. Withypoll was a relation of Sir Edward Coke's wife Lady Hatton and had been knighted by the king in 1617 at a feast held by her. His father died in 1619 and Withypoll inherited an estate of £1,100 a year, but two-thirds of this was committed to providing for his mother, three brothers and five unmarried sisters. His marriage to Jane greatly improved his financial position and in 1623 he was appointed to a post in the privy chamber of the Prince of Wales. In 1628 he became involved in a dispute between one of his brothers and an army officer. Withypoll led a group of militia from Ipswich to confront the officer. There was an exchange of fire, which resulted in one of the militiamen being shot by someone on his own side. Sir William spent a year in prison and was tried for murder, although convicted of the lesser charge of manslaughter. His friends were successful in securing him a pardon on condition that he made full reparation, but he lost his court position.

Since both George and Sir William were seriously in debt, they had a vested interest in trying to ensure their sister-in-law Bridget did not receive the third of the Reade estate she had inherited through her mother. George Villiers, duke of Buckingham, the king's favourite, meanwhile was keen to promote his various kinsmen and find them suitable brides with good fortunes. Sir William was well aware of this. It was from his own mother's house that Sir Edward Coke had dragged his fourteen-year-old daughter Frances and forced her into marriage with Buckingham's younger brother Viscount Purbeck. Buckingham identified Bridget as a suitable bride for the younger son of his sister Susan, who was married to William Feilding of Newnham Paddox. Buckingham had already ensured that the prospective bridegroom would inherit the Irish earldom of Desmond. The story within the Berkeley family was that after George lost his temper with his steward and boxed his ears, the steward got his revenge by bringing Bridget to Buckingham's attention. More prosaically Buckingham was probably aware of Bridget from the scandal surrounding her birth and recognised that she was a potentially wealthy heiress. If Buckingham did not already know Bridget's value, his sometime ally Sir Edward Coke was in a good position to inform him, while the Feildings were well-acquainted with the Berkeleys' affairs. The Berkeleys and Villiers held neighbouring manors in Leicestershire and in previous lawsuits the Berkeleys' greater wealth and higher social status had given them an advantage. Now neither of her brothers-in-law were in a position successfully to contest a lawsuit initiated on Bridget's behalf by the duke and her inheritance was secured. Her marriage to George Feilding was arranged before the duke's assassination, although it may not actually have taken place until the following year when Bridget was fourteen. After the wedding the bride went to live with the widowed Duchess of Buckingham, while her young husband travelled abroad.

With his debts mounting and his income less than he had hoped after Buckingham's intervention, George became increasingly desperate to raise money. Elizabeth and his mother meanwhile were equally concerned to defend the interests of his children. In 1630 things came to a head, when Elizabeth refused to do what George demanded and he threatened her with separation.[12] He scuttled off to France once more, leaving his mother and John Smyth to find a solution to his troubles. He was accompanied by Sir Henry Berkeley, a distant relation who acted as the family's agent in Leicestershire. Sir Henry was an elderly, scholarly man, who had developed a reputation for dealing with troublesome aristocrats. For four years he had played host to John, viscount Purbeck, whose fragile mental health broke down when his wife Frances was charged with adultery. Now Sir Henry took on the responsibility of setting up George in an appropriate, frugal style in France. This proved a difficult task, leading George's mother to thunderously complain by letter of George's extravagance.[13]

George's young wife proved to be a stubborn negotiator on behalf of herself and her children, causing John Smyth to despair of getting her agreement. Since George needed a speedy solution to his money troubles, he instructed Smyth to seek one that did not touch his wife's lands.[14] Among the property disposed of was Caludon castle, which had remained an important symbol of the Berkeley presence in the Midlands even as his grandfather and father had disposed of so much of their land there. During George's absence Smyth worried about the effect on his children of the melancholy atmosphere of his wife's household in St John's Lane, 'where nothing raignes but murmures and discontent'.[15] He also disapproved of George's plan to resolve some of his financial troubles by arranging the marriage of his nine-year-old son and heir Charles to an unnamed, older woman. Eventually in 1633 the difficulty of sorting everything out from a distance brought George back to England. At Christmas there was a fresh crisis. Elizabeth ended up at Wymondham, Sir Henry Berkeley's house in Leicestershire. Like Viscount Purbeck, Elizabeth was placed there under royal protection after a final, presumably violent, rift with George, while the details of their separation could be sorted out. The couple were never to live together again.

In the last years of her life George's mother took advantage of her renewed control of the Berkeley finances during his absence abroad to syphon off some of the money for her own use. The £3,000 which she divided between two of her kinswomen was about twice her yearly income from the estate. No doubt she felt it was reasonable, given the sacrifices she had made for the Berkeleys, that she should recoup some of her losses to the advantage of her birth family. It did, however, sour Smyth's view of the 'honorable, vertuous and prudent' woman he had worked with for so many years.[16] Elizabeth died in 1635 at the age of fifty eight and was buried at Cranford. The inscription on her funeral monument described her relationship through her father to Queen Elizabeth, but did not mention either of her husbands or her children. The heraldry included the Berkeley and Carey arms and quarterings, but not Chamberlain. The monument reinforces the impression of Elizabeth as a thoroughly independent matriarch.

6 End of an Era

Following his mother's death, it was Lord Berkeley's estranged wife and his sister Theophila who took over the reins of the family's affairs with Smyth's assistance. His mother had left Cranford to her younger grandson George and, since Theophila and her husband had no children, it was agreed that they should adopt her nephew. George consequently went to live with his aunt and uncle at Durdans. Also living there since being orphaned in 1629 were Sir Robert's twelve-year-old nephew Robert and eight-year-old niece Theophila. These cousins, who were presumably the couple's godchildren, would later marry. In 1634 George's aunt had also been entrusted with the care of Elizabeth, the teenage daughter of her cousin Sir John Zouch. In an attempt to repair the family fortunes Sir John had finally sold Codnor castle and emigrated to Virginia with his son and eldest daughter, leaving his two younger daughters behind in England. At Durdans George found a relief from the strained atmosphere of his childhood that gave the house a special place in his affections. Once their income and possession of Durdans was confirmed on his father's death in 1634, Sir Robert and Theophila had set about extending the house, adding a single storey, flat roofed, long gallery in classical style. They also installed formal gardens with a parterre, fountains and statues. A painting by Jacob Knyff, now at Berkeley castle, shows this house in 1673, a few years before it was demolished. Here the young Samuel Pepys was brought by his uncle, who worked for Sir Robert, and co-opted to act in a private production of Beaumont and Fletcher's romantic comedy Philaster, or Love Lies a-Bleeding. It was a very different atmosphere from that which reigned in the melancholy household in St John's Lane during George's early childhood.[1]

Theophila was also involved in the negotiation of her brother's daughter Elizabeth's marriage to another of her husband's nephews, Edward, the eldest son of Sir Robert's younger brother John. Like all Sir Edward Coke's sons John had been provided with a substantial estate and had married Meriel Wheatley, the heiress to Holkham in Norfolk. Edward, who was about ten years older than Elizabeth, was the eldest of John and Meriel's six sons and nine daughters. He was the prospective heir of both his father and, since Sir Robert had no children, his uncle. The marriage appears to have taken place at around the time of his mother's death in the summer of 1636, although the couple would not have co-habited until Elizabeth was older. Concluding the marriage was a way of securing Elizabeth's right to a marriage portion of £5,000 from her father. George was not actually in a position to provide the lump sum, but he did pay annual interest which ensured she had some income.

In 1637 Lord Berkeley sold the manor of Bosham in Sussex to his younger son, thus ensuring that it stayed in the family. Theophila proved to be as skilful a negotiator as her mother and grandmother. She refused to pay over the odds for the property, even if it was to help her brother out of his difficulties.[2] Lord Berkeley's debts and his sales of land made it difficult to find a bride for his heir Charles. The problem was exacerbated by the sale of Caludon, which had provided the family with appropriately aristocratic accommodation for three generations. During the previous decades they had made little use of Berkeley castle and the accommodation there was not up to modern standards. As it was in her son's interest, Lady Berkeley authorised the necessary improvements to the fabric and furnishing of the castle, so there would be an appropriate country residence to show prospective fathers-in-law.[3] Charles meanwhile continued his education. Then in January 1641 tragedy struck, when aged seventeen he was drowned while crossing the Channel to France. His death changed the family's fortunes, as the fourteen-year-old George became the heir to the barony and the separate property that had been secured for him would eventually be returned to the main estate. Charles's death was a particularly heavy blow for his mother, who had already handed the care of George over to Theophila. The following month the indefatigable Smyth, who had managed the family's affairs for so many years, died after a short illness. His eldest son, also John, who had been assisting his father for several years, now took over his father's role.

By March 1641 Theophila was engaged with the help of the younger John Smyth in negotiating a marriage for her nephew George. The proposed bride was Elizabeth, the only daughter of Thomas, viscount Somerset, the younger son of the Earl of Worcester. Her mother Helen had previously been the third and final wife of Ormond, the Irish magnate whose first countess was Theophila's great-aunt Elizabeth. Somerset's estate at Badminton, which his daughter would in due course inherit, offered a means of making up for the Berkeley property that had been lost and would consolidate the family's position in Gloucestershire. The prospective bride was probably a little older than George, but she was not the aged woman that Smyth had feared his father would force upon his elder brother. The only negative aspect to the proposed match from the Berkeley viewpoint was the Somerset family's catholicism, which meant there was a theoretical danger that the viscount could be convicted of recusancy and his lands seized. As the Irish rebelled in the autumn of 1641, this became a more immediate concern. Meanwhile, the Somerset side were worried that any financial settlement might be overturned by Lord Berkeley falling into further debt. Negotiations proceeded for some time, but eventually came to nothing.[4]

As the country slid towards civil war, Lord Berkeley attempted to maintain good relations with both sides. He was then living in Clerkenwell and continued to attend the House of Lords after the withdrawal of the king. At the same time he assured the royalists of his support, while pleading ill-health to justify not taking an active part in hostilities. Berkeley castle was garrisoned by parliament in 1642, but abandoned the following year when the king arrived in the area to besiege Gloucester. After Bristol was taken by parliament in 1645, there was a fear that Berkeley castle would be demolished. George's continued attendance of the House of Lords then paid off, as he was able to successfully petition for the castle to be preserved and used as a parliamentary garrison. He was also allowed to arrange for his own papers to be removed from the castle for safe keeping. The following year the House of Commons did order some of the walls and gates around the castle to be demolished, but the destruction was limited. Lord Berkeley continued to attend parliament until the House of Lords was abolished in 1649.

Sir Robert Coke meanwhile was imprisoned in the Tower as a royalist and his estate was confiscated, although he successfully petitioned for Theophila to receive an income for her maintenance. Theophila was able to visit her husband in prison until her death from smallpox in the spring of 1643. Sir Robert was finally released in 1646, after having paid a substantial fine. In November 1652 he was appointed to be sheriff of Suffolk, an office which required the holder to reside in the county except under exceptional circumstances. The writing of his will in December 1652 suggests that he was already ill and may have obtained an exemption.[5] He died in July 1653. As previously agreed, he left Durdans to his nephew George, while the bulk of his estate passed to his brother John. As his executor he appointed Edward Wenyeve, who succeeded him as sheriff of Suffolk. Sir Robert had purchased a house on land adjoining Durdans, where he hoped his executor would establish a library for the use of local clergymen. In the event his books remained at Durdans, possibly because Wenyeve died in 1658 before the library could be established. They were given to Sion College in 1682. Sir Robert asked to be buried at Epsom, as close to his wife's grave as possible. George subsequently erected a monument to his aunt and uncle in the church.

Theophila's death deprived her nephew of one of the stalwart defenders of his interests and an important source of advice. In 1645 John Smyth the younger advised him that he needed a rich wife to preserve what remained of the Berkeley estate. His father's debts were now so great, that unless there was an injection of cash, more land would have to be sold. The chosen bride was Elizabeth, elder daughter of John Massingberd, a wealthy merchant and treasurer of the East India Company. Her mother Cecilia was also from a London merchant background. This was not a match that George's great-grandmother with her Howard pride would have contemplated for a moment, but the economic case for marrying money was strong. Her three brothers having died, Elizabeth and her younger sister Mary would between them inherit their father's considerable estate. The civil war had also made George aware of how uncertain income from land could be. His father had made some tentative colonial investments before the war, but George was to be the first Berkeley to become closely involved in trade and colonial matters. His father-in-law's advice and contacts were to be invaluable in making this transition.

Elizabeth Massingberd and George Berkeley were married at Morden, Surrey in August 1646. As part of the marriage agreement the bride's father took over the management of the estate. He ordered all rents and other payments to be paid to him and began to look into the exploitation of the woods, parks and other sources of income. Lord Berkeley was obliged to live on an allowance of £800 a year, which forced him to reduce the size of his household. It was expected

End of an Era

that he would go abroad, but living on a restricted income among the exiled royalists held few attractions. George's mother, who had been living with her daughter and son-in-law, was moved to cheaper lodgings. Attempts were made to persuade her to agree to surrender her rights and inheritance in return for an annuity. She refused and, having endured years of unhappy marriage and preserved her interests against her husband, Lady Berkeley proved more than a match for George's father-in-law.

The brief reign of John Massingberd, who died in 1653, helped to put the Berkeley finances back on track. The old baronial traditions and profligate ways were replaced by more commercial considerations. The paternalism of John Smyth's management gave way to more extensive exploitation of the estate's resources. Lord Berkeley died at the house in St John's Lane in 1658. He was buried in Cranford, while his son erected a monument to him at Epsom. His funeral sermon was preached by John Pearson, the future bishop of Chester who had been chaplain to Sir Robert Coke at Durdans.[6] His daughter Elizabeth was by then a childless widow. She died in 1661. The dowager Lady Berkeley lived to see her son settle into a fruitful, apparently happy marriage. When she died in 1669, the land she had inherited finally became available to the family. Most of it was sold very quickly. A decade later George had secured the family fortunes and was created Earl of Berkeley.

Notes

The essential source for this book has been John Smyth's *Lives of the Berkeleys*. The context of the production of this first English genealogical history are discussed in J. Broadway, *'No historie so meete'* (2006). I have made extensive use of biographies from the *Oxford Dictionary of National Biography* and the *History of Parliament*. For House of Lords attendance see the *Journal of the House of Lords* [http://www.british-history.ac.uk/lords-jrnl/vol1] and for events related to the court A.F. Pollard ed., *Tudor Tracts, 1532-1588* (1903) and J. Nichols, *The progresses and public processions of Queen Elizabeth* (1823) and *The progresses, processions, and magnificent festivities, of King James* (1828).

Other sources are included in the chapter notes.

Abbreviations

BL	British Library
GA	Gloucestershire Archives
HMC	Historical Manuscripts Commission
Jeayes	I.H. Jeayes, *Descriptive Catalogue of the Charters and Muniments at Berkeley Castle* (Bristol, 1892)
L&P	J.S Brewer et al, *Letters & Papers Foreign and Domestic, Henry VIII* (1862-1932)
Lives	Sir John Maclean ed., *The Lives of the Berkeleys*, vol. 2 (1883)
TNA	The National Archives

Preface

N. Clark, *Gender, Family and Politics* (2018); B.J. Harris, *English Aristocratic Women 1450-1550* (2002); R. Hutchinson, *House of Treason* (2009).

[1] *Lives*, 229.

1 The Savage Marriage

D.M. Head, *The Ebbs and Flows of Fortune* (1995); E. W. Ives, *Anne Boleyn* (1986); E.W. Ives, 'Crime, Sanctuary, and Royal Authority under Henry VIII: The Exemplary Sufferings of the Savage Family' in Morris S. Arnold ed., *On the Laws and Customs of England* (1981); D. MacCulloch, *Thomas Cromwell* (2018); H. Miller, *Henry VIII and the English Nobility* (1986); B.A. Murphy, *Bastard Prince* (2001); M. St Clare

Notes

Byrne ed., *The Lisle Letters* (1983); S. Thurley, *Houses of Power* (2017).

[1] *Lives,* 267
[2] I.H. Jeayes, *Descriptive Catalogue of the Gresley Family* (1895), 102-3, 105; Derbyshire Archives, D77/1/61/1.
[3] *L&P,* vol. 5, 327.
[4] TNA, PROB 11/21/237.
[5] T.B. Howell ed., *State Trials* vol. 1 (1816), 292.
[6] *Lives*, 393.
[7] J. Rhodes ed., *The Terrier of Llanthony Priory's Houses and Lands in Gloucester* (2016), 146.
[8] *Lives*, 245; TNA, PROB 11/25/28.
[9] *Lives*, 252; John Stow, *Annales of England* (1605), 946.
[10] *L&P,* vol. 6, 314-5.
[11] Jeayes, 209.
[12] *L&P,* vol. 7, 635.

2 A Widow and Her Children

E.W. Ives, 'Court and County Palatine in the Reign of Henry VIII: the Career of William Brereton of Malpas', *Transactions of the Historic Society of Lancashire and Cheshire* 123 (1972), 1-38.

[1] *Lives*, 267.
[2] *L&P,* vol. 9, 12.
[3] *L&P,* vol. 11, 418.
[4] *L&P,* vol. 13, Part 2, 542.
[5] *L&P,* vol. 13, Part 1, 12.
[6] TNA, SP 11/1.
[7] *Lives*, 281.
[8] TNA, PROB 11/37/171; *Lives*, 382.
[9] J.G. Nichols ed., *The Diary of Henry Machyn* (1848), 70.
[10] Jeayes, 215.
[11] S. Lang & M. McGregor eds., *Tudor Wills Proved in Bristol* (1993), 97-9.
[12] BL, MS Cotton Titus BII, 349; *Journal of the Historical & Archaeological Association of Ireland* 3rd series 1 (1869), 543.

3 Mary Queen of Scots and the Howards

Z. Dovey, *An Elizabethan Progress* (1996); E.P. Shirley, *Stemmata Shirleiana* (1873); A. Somerset, *Elizabeth I* (1991).

[1] N. Williams, *Tudor* Tragedy (1964), 165.
[2] ibid, 170-2.
[3] A. Clifford ed., *State Papers & Letters of Sir Ralph Sadler* (1809), 405-6.
[4] Williams, *Tudor Tragedy*, 214.
[5] *Lives*, 384.
[6] *Lives*, 278.
[7] *Lives*, 291.
[8] *Lives*, 403.
[9] BL, Lansdowne 59, 169-72.
[10] HMC, *Calendar of the Manuscripts of the Marquis of Bath*, vol. 5 (1980), 83.
[11] W. Fordyce, *History and Antiquities of the County Palatine of Durham*, vol. 2 (1857), 103.
[12] *Lives*, 402.

4 Careys and Townshends

S. Adams, *Leicester and the Court* (2002); K. Bundesen, "No other faction but my own':Dynastic Politics and Elizabeth I's Carey Cousins' (PhD thesis, University of Nottingham, 2008); B. Cobbing & P. Priestland, *Sir Thomas Stanhope of Shelford* (2003); C. Laoutaris, *Shakespeare and the Countess* (2014).

[1] *Lives*, 395.
[2] Berkeley Castle Muniments, GL5/129; K. Duncan-Jones, 'Bess Carey's Petrarch: newly discovered Elizabethan sonnets', *Review of English Studies*, n.s. 50 (1999), 304-19.
[3] Jeayes, 330.
[4] TNA, PROB 11/88/71.
[5] *Lives*, 338.
[6] *Lives*, 370.
[7] TNA, PROB 11/77/149.
[8] *Lives*, 393.
[9] TNA PROB 11/111/228.
[10] TNA, PROB 11/102/245.
[11] GA, D8887/2, 38 & 41.
[12] BL, Add MS 33588, 50-55; GA, D8887/3, 6.

Notes

5 Cokes and Stanhopes

L. Campbell, 'Sir Roger Townshend and His Family: a Study of Gentry Life in Early Seventeenth Century Norfolk' (PhD thesis, University of East Anglia, 1990); C. W. James, *Chief Justice Coke, his family & descendants at Holkham* (1929).

[1] N.G. McClure ed., *The Letters of John Chamberlain*, vol. 1 (1939), 54.
[2] *Lives*, 426.
[3] TNA, PROB 11/139/119.
[4] TNA, PROB 11/123/687.
[5] TNA, PROB 11/166/395.
[6] TNA, PROB 11/131/287.
[7] BL, Add MS 41655, 59.
[8] GA, D8887/3, 10.
[9] W.R. Prest ed, *The Diary of Sir Richard Hutton* (1991), 60.
[10] TNA, PROB 11/151/230.
[11] GA, D8887/3, 12.
[12] GA, D8887/2, 58.
[13] GA, D8887/2, 71; D8887/9, 103; D8887/16, 21.
[14] GA, D8887/2, 73.
[15] GA, D8887/9, 111.
[16] GA, D9125/1/6950; Sir J. Maclean ed., *A History of the Hundred of Berkeley* (1885), 408.

6 End of an Era

H. Durant, *The Somerset Sequence* (1976); L. Stone, *Family and Fortune* (1973).

[1] *Virginia Magazine of History and Biography* 12 (1904), 87-9; C. Tomalin, *Samuel Pepys, The Unequalled Self* (2002), 10-11.
[2] GA, D8887/5, 30; D8887/10, 67.
[3] GA, D8887/10, 111.
[4] GA, D8887/16, 10, 12; BL, Add MS 33588, 60.
[5] TNA, PROB 11/230/446.
[6] John Pearson, *The Patriarchal Funeral* (1658).

Index

Aragon, Catherine of 1, 2, 10, 12, 15, 22, 29
Arnold, John 14, 17
Arnold (Rowdon/Berkeley), Cicely x, 13-14, 17-18, 28, 33, 38
Ashwood, Henry 78
Audley (Dudley, Howard), Margaret xii, 36, 38
Aylworth, Francis 51
Bacon, Francis 68, 70; Sir Nathaniel 68, 81; Sir Nicholas 68
Bacon (Townshend), Anne xiv, 68, 72
Barlow, John 26
Berkeley, Charles x, 83, 86, 88; Edward x, 49, 50; Ferdinand 38-9; George, lord Berkeley viii, x, xiv, 71, 75, 78, 79-80, 81, 82, 83, 84, 85-6, 87, 88, 89, 91; George, earl of Berkeley x, 83, 87, 88, 89, 90, 91; Henry, lord Berkeley vii, x, xii, 23, 28, 32, 33, 34, 35, 37, 38-9, 40, 47, 49, 50-1, 53, 54, 56, 59, 60, 62-3, 64, 65-6, 67, 68-70, 71, 73, 74, 76, 78; Sir Henry 85, 86; James 21, 24; Sir James x, 7, 8, 9; Jane 39, 50; John 11; Katherine 38-9; Maurice (d. 1506) x, 5-7, 8; Maurice, lord Berkeley x, 6, 8, 9, 10-11, 13; Maurice (d. 1547) x, 9, 14, 17-18, 22, 24, 26-7; Thomas, lord Berkeley (d. 1533) x, 7, 8, 9-10, 11, 12, 13-14, 16-17; Thomas, lord Berkeley (d. 1534) x, 1, 5, 8- 22, 23-4; Sir Thomas x, 51, 55, 58, 60, 62-3, 64-5, 70, 71, 72-4, 75; William, marquess Berkeley x, 5-6
Berkeley (Berkeley), Katherine x, 6-7, 9, 11, 12
Berkeley (Butler), Elizabeth x, 33, 37-8, 40-1, 88
Berkeley (Coke), Elizabeth x, xiv, 83, 87-8, 91; Theophila x, 64-5, 75, 76, 77, 82, 87, 88, 89, 90
Berkeley (Denys), Anne x, 9
Berkeley (Shirley), Frances x, 38, 49, 56
Berkeley (Throckmorton), Mirriel x, 13
Berkeley (Zouch), Mary 35, 49-50, 54, 59
Boleyn, Anne xiii, 1, 5, 11, 14-16, 19-20, 22, 23, 26, 32, 66
Bott, John 52-3, 57-8
Brandon, Charles, duke of Suffolk 3, 15, 28
Brandon (Grey), Frances 28
Brereton, William 5, 21, 25, 26
Bristol 16, 28, 29, 37, 41, 89
Brooke, George 78-9; William, lord Cobham 64
Browne, Sir Matthew 72
Browne (Somerset), Elizabeth 5, 20
Buckinghamshire, Burnham Abbey 45; Stoke Poges 14, 16
Burgh (Brooke, Reade), Elizabeth 78-9
Butler, Thomas, earl of Ormond x, 37-8, 40-1, 88
Calais 9-11, 13, 14, 15-16, 17, 19, 22, 25

Carey, George, lord Hunsdon xiii, 60-3, 64, 71-2; Henry, lord Hunsdon xiii, 60-1, 64; John, lord Hunsdon 63, 72; Sir Robert 71

Carey (Berkeley, Chamberlain), Elizabeth viii, x, xiii, 60-5, 70-5, 76, 78, 79, 82-3, 85, 86, 87

Carey (Howard), Katherine xi, xiii, 60, 61

Carey (Scrope), Philadelphia xiii, 60

catholic recusancy 39, 42-6, 53, 55-6, 58, 65, 89

Cecil, Sir Robert 64, 72, 77; Thomas, earl of Exeter 76, 78; William, lord Burghley 47, 48

Cecil (Hatton, Coke), Elizabeth xiv, 76-7, 78, 82, 84

Cecil (Read), Mildred 78

Chamberlain, Thomas 82-3

Charles I 71, 89

Cleves, Anne of 30

Coke, Edward xiv, 87; Sir Edward xiv, 76-7, 84-5, 87; John xiv, 87; Robert 87; Sir Robert x, xiv, 76-7, 87, 89-90; Theophila 87

Constable, Sir Marmaduke 7, 8, 9

Constable (Ingilby, Berkeley), Eleanor x, 7, 8, 9, 13

Council, of the North 25, 75; of Wales 39, 67

Coventry 23, 29, 40, 46, 52, 55, 57, 63, 69, 74, 75, 77, 78

Cromwell, Thomas 5, 19, 20, 21, 22, 24, 25, 26, 28, 30

Cumberland, Carlisle 39, 42; Workington 42

Dacre, William, lord Dacre 22

Dacre (Howard), Anne xii, 45, 53-4, 55-6; Elizabeth xii, 53

Denny, Sir Anthony 36

Derby, Robert 21

Deryshire, Bretby 54; Codnor 54, 59, 71, 87; Derby 55

Devereux, Robert, earl of Essex 64; Walter, earl of Essex xiii, 52

Douglas (Howard), Margaret xi, 25, 32

Dudley, Ambrose, earl of Warwick 36, 49, 52, 58; Guildford, 36; Henry, 36; John, duke of Northumberland 36, 49, 66; Robert, earl of Leicester xiii, 38, 40, 49-53, 56, 57-8

duelling 70, 72

Durham, Brancepeth 46; Durham 46, 58;

education, female 32, 61, 67, 75

Edward VI 30, 32, 33, 36, 37, 66

Egerton, Sir Thomas 65

Elizabeth I 36-7, 38, 39, 40, 42, 44-5, 47-8, 50, 51-2, 53-4, 60, 63, 68, 71

Essex 70; Audley End 36 48, 51

Eure, Ralph, lord Eure 74-5

Feilding, Basil 69; George, earl of Desmond xiv, 84-5

Fenn, Humphrey 57

Field of Cloth of Gold 10-11, 13, 16, 22

Fitzalan, Henry, earl of Arundel 33,
44, 53

Fitzalan (Howard), Mary xii, 33, 35

Fitzroy, Henry, duke of Richmond xii, 1, 15, 25, 26
Flodden, battle of 9, 29
foreign travel, as education 70
Foxe, John 32, 33
France 2, 3-4, 9, 11, 13, 15-16, 19, 22, 36, 37, 39, 73, 74, 83, 85, 88
Francis I 10, 15
Francis, duc d'Alençon/d'Anjou 51, 52, 53
funeral ceremonies 12, 16, 34, 36, 58, 63-4, 69, 82, 91; monuments 64, 86, 90, 91
Gawdy, Thomas 31
Gloucestershire vii, 5, 9, 11-12, 14, 17, 19, 24, 34, 38, 50, 63, 71, 74; Badminton 88; Berkeley vii, 5, 6, 8, 9, 12, 17, 20, 24, 33, 35, 50, 74, 87, 88, 89; Gloucester 14, 26, 27, 89; Mangotsfield 9-10, 14, 16-18, 23-4, 26, 27, 29, 35; Saintbury 29; Stoke Gifford x, 6, 11; Tewkesbury 2; Thornbury 12, 24; Westbury-on-Trym 26; Yate 6, 9-10, 11-12, 17, 22, 23, 24, 26, 28, 29, 34, 35, 38-9
Goodrich, Thomas, bishop of Ely 29
Gresley, George 4, 20, 27; William 4
Grey, Henry, marquess of Dorset 28
Grey (Dudley), Lady Jane 36
Grey (Sutton), Cecily 28
Habsburg, Archduke Charles 38
Hampshire, Beaurepaire 54
Hart, Sir Eustace 80
Hastings, Francis 19, 20, 22; George, earl of Huntingdon 13, 19, 22
Hastings (Berkeley), Mary x, 13, 14, 18
Henry VII 2, 6, 8, 61
Henry VIII xi, xiii, 1, 2, 8, 9, 10, 12, 15-16, 25, 29, 30, 37, 52, 61
Herbert, Henry, earl of Pembroke 62
Hertfordshire 31; Hunsdon 61
Holland, Elizabeth 16, 31; Philemon 75
horoscopes, casting of 52, 56
Howard, Charles, earl of Nottingham xi, xiii, 32, 60, 67, 71, 72; Henry, earl of Northampton xii, 45, 48, 51, 53, 72, 78, 79; Henry, earl of Surrey xii, 15, 30-1, 32, 33, 34, 50; John, 1st duke of Norfolk xi, 6; Philip, earl of Arundel xii, 35, 45, 48, 51, 53, 55, 56, 58, 59, 67; Thomas, 2nd duke of Norfolk xi, 6, 8, 9, 12; Thomas, 3rd duke of Norfolk xi, xii, 12, 13, 14-16, 17, 18, 19, 25, 26, 30-1, 32, 33, 34; Thomas, 4th duke of Norfolk xii, 31, 32, 33, 36, 38-9, 42-5, 47-8, 49, 67; Thomas, earl of Arundel 55, 79; Thomas, earl of Suffolk xii, 53, 72. 79; William (d. 1640) xii, 53; William, lord Howard of Effingham xi, 18, 31
Howard (Berkeley), Katherine x, xii, 33, 34-6, 37, 38-40, 45, 47, 48, 49-51, 52-3, 55, 57-9, 60, 62-4, 65, 69, 72, 73, 79
Howard (de Vere), Anne xi, 20

98

Howard (Fitzroy), Mary xii, 15, 26, 30, 31-2
Howard (Neville), Jane xii, 37, 39, 44-8, 50, 58
Howard (Scrope), Margaret xii, 39, 43, 44, 60
Howard (Sheffield), Douglas xi, 32, 50, 52
Howard (Stanley), Katherine 12-13
Howard (Tudor), Katherine xi, 30
hunting 33, 35, 38, 44, 46, 50
Ingilby, William 8, 9
inns of court 12, 37; Gray's Inn 66, 81
Ireland 17, 37-8, 40, 52
Isle of Wight 62
Italy 73, 74, 83
James I 71, 72, 73, 78, 81
jointure 7-8
Kent 34, 63, 73; Stone 22
Knollys, Sir Francis xiii, 42
Knollys (Devereux, Dudley), Lettice xiii, 52, 53, 60
Leicestershire 4, 19, 38, 63, 85; Croxton 21, 23-4; Hoby 29; Seagrave 29; Sileby 56; Staunton Harold 56; Wymondham 86
Leigh, Sir Thomas 62
Leyburne (Dacre, Howard), Elizabeth xii, 42-3
Lisle, viscount See Sidney, Talbot
London 12, 21, 22, 29, 30-1, 33, 34, 35-6, 37, 40, 47, 51, 53, 56, 57, 58, 61, 62, 66, 67, 78, 82, 90; Barbican 66, 68-9, 79, 80 Blackfriars 61, 63, 64, 73, 75, 82; Clerkenwell 79-80, 86, 87, 89, 91; Tower 3, 6, 19-20, 25, 26, 30, 31, 32, 36, 45, 47, 48, 55, 58, 66, 89
Mary I 15, 32, 36, 37, 49, 66
Mary of Guise 32
Mary, Queen of Scots 42-5, 47, 54, 55, 56, 58
Massingberd, John 90-1
Massingberd (Berkeley), Elizabeth x, 90
Middlesex 73; Cranford 82, 83, 86, 87, 91; Kensington 72; Osterley 78
Mowbray, inheritance x, xi, 6, 23
Neville, Charles, earl of Westmorland xii, 39, 44-7, 58
Norfolk 67, 70, 76, 81; Castle Rising 35; Holkham 87; Kenninghall 30-1, 34, 40, 45, 51, 58; Norwich 51; Raynham 48; Stiffkey 68; Thetford 12
Nottinghamshire, Shelford 54, 66; Welbeck 21
Oxfordshire, Ricote 31
parliament 6, 11, 17, 21, 36, 47, 71, 77, 89
Paston (Coke), Bridget 76
Pauncefote, John 3
Pearson, John 91
Percy, Thomas, earl of Northumberland 42, 46
Perrot, Thomas 11
Philip of Spain 33, 35
Phines, William 57
Poyntz, Sir Nicholas (d. 1556) x, 13, 16, 18, 24, 26; Sir Nicholas (d. 1585) 39, 50
Preston (Leyburne), Helen 42-3
Radcliffe, Jane 65; Henry, 2nd earl

of Sussex xi, 23; Henry, viscount Fitzwalter 79; Robert, 1st earl of Sussex 23; Thomas, 3rd earl of Sussex 40, 46

Rawson (Stanhope), Anne xiv, 66

Reade, Francis 78-9; Thomas 78; Sir William 78, 83

Reade (Stanhope), Anne xiv, 78-9

rebellion, Wyatt's 33-4, 36, 37; Northern earls 44-5, 46, 47

Rowdon (Berkeley), Frances x, 14

royal residences, Greenwich 1, 14, 19, 34, 37; Hampton Court 72; Nonsuch 66, 82; Whitehall 1, 53, 82; Windsor 14, 15, 45

Russell, Sir Thomas 45, 48

Russell (Dudley), Anne 51, 61, 62, 73

Sandys, William, lord Sandys 11

Savage, Christopher 29; Sir Christopher 9; George 29; John, 29; Sir John (d. 1492) 2; Sir John (d. 1527) 2-4, 8; Sir John (d. 1528) 2-4, 5; Sir John (d. 1597) 54; Thomas, archbishop of York 2

Savage (Berkeley), Anne x, 1-5, 16, 18-22, 23,4, 26-9, 33, 35, 40, 49

Scotland 39, 42, 43, 46, 47, 55, 60, 71

Scrope, Henry, lord Scrope xii, 39, 42, 44; Thomas, lord Scrope xiii, 60

Senhouse, William, bishop of Durham 8

Seymour, Edward, duke of Somerset 30, 37, 66; Sir Thomas 30, 36

Shirley, George x, 56; Sir Thomas 54

Sidney, Sir Philip 49-50; Robert, viscount Lisle 49-50, 73

Smyth, John the elder vii, viii, 12, 13, 17, 18, 23, 29, 34, 35, 45, 49, 53, 54, 55, 56, 63, 65, 69, 73-4, 76, 85-6, 87, 88, 89, 91; John the younger 88, 90; Richard 29

Somerset 5, 32, 35, 63; Portbury 77

Somerset, Charles, 1st earl of Worcester 2, 3-4, 5, 10, 27; Elizabeth 88-9; Henry, 2nd earl of Worcester 5.

Somerset (Savage, Brereton), Elizabeth 2, 3, 5, 20, 24, 25

Spelman, John xiv, 81-2

Spencer, Sir John 60, 62; Sir Thomas 62, 79

Spencer (Carey, Eure), Elizabeth xiii, 60-1, 74-5

Spencer (Stanley, Egerton), Alice 61, 65

Stafford, Anthony 83; Edward, duke of Buckingham 12, 13, 30, 39

Stafford (Howard), Elizabeth xii, 12, 16, 18, 31

Stanhope, Edward, 69; Sir Michael (d. 1552) xiv, 66; Sir Michael (d. 1621) xiv, 69, 78-9

Stanhope (Berkeley), Elizabeth viii, x, xiv, 78-80, 83-4, 85-6, 87, 88, 90-1

Stanhope (Feilding), Bridget xiv, 80, 84-5

Stanhope (Radcliffe, Withypoll), Jane xiv, 79, 84

Stanhope (Townshend, Berkeley), Jane x, xiv, 66-71, 72, 77, 78, 80-2
Stanley, Ferdinand, earl of Derby 61, 65
Steyning, Thomas 32
Suffolk 67, 73, 89-90; Earl Soham 32; Framlingham 31; Huntingfield 77; Ipswich 84; Sudbourne 78
Surrey vii; Beddington 66; Durdans (Epsom) 82, 87, 90, 91; Morden, 90; Reigate 31; Walton-on-Thames 72
Sussex 17, 33, 63; Bosham 88; Wiston 54
Sutton, Edward 27-8
Sutton (Somerset), Eleanor 5, 27
Talbot, Thomas, viscount Lisle 5
Tauke (Gresley, Savage), Alice 4, 20, 27
Throckmorton, Francis 56; Sir John 56; Robert x, 13
Townshend, Sir John xiv, 68, 70, 72; Sir Roger (d. 1590), xiv, 48, 54, 66, 67-8; Sir Roger (d. 1615) xiv, 68, 70, 80; Sir Roger bart., xiv, 80-1; Stanhope xiv, 81
Townshend (Spelman), Anne xiv, 81-2
Try, Gerard 29; Thomas 23, 28
Tudor (Brandon), Mary 3, 9, 16, 28, 61
universities, Cambridge 51, 66, 67, 81; Oxford 37, 55, 57, 58, 60, 78, 82
Vaux, Sir Nicholas 11, 13
Veel (Berkeley), Susan x, 7, 8
de Vere (Howard, Steyning), Frances xii, 15, 30, 32, 35, 38
de Vere (Willoughby, Hart), Mary 80
Villiers, George, duke of Buckingham 84-5; John, viscount Purbeck xiv, 84, 85, 86
violence, use of 2-3, 21-2, 26-7, 79, 84
Wade, Christopher 57-9
wardship 7-8, 23, 45, 72, 78, 79, 83
Warwickshire vii, 13, 36, 38, 58, 68; Caludon 23, 24, 28-9, 35, 37, 38, 39, 40, 50, 51, 54, 56, 62, 63, 64, 74, 75, 77, 85, 88; Claverdon 62, 74; Dunchurch 62; Newnham Paddox 84; Stoneleigh 62; Thurlaston 62
Wentworth, Thomas, lord Wentworth 31
Wenyeve, Edward 90
Westminster, 1, 20, 21, 64
Wheatley (Coke), Meriel xiv, 87
White, John, bishop of Lincoln 33
Williams, Sir John 31
Wiltshire, Bridget 22, 25; Sir John 22
Withypoll, Sir William xiv, 84
Wolsey, Cardinal Thomas 2-3, 4, 5, 15
Worcestershire, Elmley Castle 2, 29; Hanley Castle 2; Strensham 45
Yorkshire 9; Bolton 42, 43, 44; Cawood 46; Flamborough 7; Hovingham 8; Ripley 7
Zouch, Elizabeth 87; Sir John (d. 1611) x, 54, 59, 71; Sir John (d. 1639), 87